The Apostle Paul

The persecutor, preacher, and church planter

Don Pruett

Other Books by Don Pruett

- Come and Believe

  (Based on the Gospel of John
  and the New Testament books
  of Peter and James)

- Victory over Death

  (Based on the Gospel of Luke)

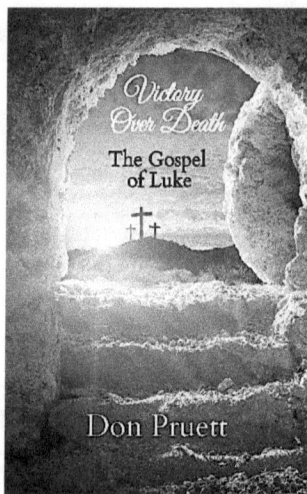

Don Pruett

Publisher: Hoot Books Publishing, 851 French Moore Boulevard, Suite 136, Abingdon VA 24211.

Scripture quotations are from the King James Version (KJV) of the Holy Bible. Commentaries and other translations used for research include:

- NIV Zondervan Study Bible Commentary, copyright 2015 by Zondervan, Grand Rapids Michigan. Materials used are within the publisher's limits that do not require prior written permission for usage.
- Thompson's Chain Reference Bible (KJV), third improved edition, copyright 1934, published by B. B. Kirkbride Bible Company, Inc., Indianapolis, Indiana. Verses quoted in this book fall within the publisher's guidelines for usage without prior consent.
- The Thompson's Chain Reference Study Bible, New King James Version (NKJV), copyright 1995, publisher B. B. Kirkbride Bible Company, Inc., Indianapolis Indiana. The verses quoted in this book fall within the publisher's guidelines for usage without prior consent.

ISBN: 978-1-959700-02-9

Don Pruett

Contents

Part One

Paul's Missionary Journeys

Introduction

The formal introduction to Saul, a Roman citizen, is outlined in Chapter One of this book. He was born in a Jewish and God-fearing home in Tarsus, Turkey. Saul was able to obtain an advanced education so he could learn all about Jewish laws and customs.

Saul's miraculous conversion to Christ occurred under most unusual circumstances. The powerful message from heaven caused Saul to make a complete change in his mission and life's work. His life was transformed by God from being a persecutor of Christians to become a preacher to make more Christians. Many believed and Paul planted New Testament churches wherever he traveled.

Before Saul was converted, he was fearless as he frequently had Christians arrested because of their faith. Persecution of believers ran throughout Saul's mission like an ugly thread. His goal was to make life impossible for Christ followers and drive them back to Judaism.

After Saul accepted Christ he became an example for every child of God, showing us what it is to face life without fear. His name was changed to Paul, and he was never ashamed to preach Jesus as the risen Lord. Our faith in God helps overcome the fears that creep into our daily life as we move from one problem to another.

Paul wrote letters of instruction and encouragement to the new churches he planted. He wanted them to keep their faith in Christ so their churches would flourish.

Paul gives us the hope of resurrection due to Christ being brought forth from death.

Chapter One

Saul's Introduction

<u>Saul's Early Adult Years</u>

Saul was born around 5BC to 5AD in the metropolitan city of Tarsus in southern Turkey. Tarsus is located about twelve miles inland from the Mediterranean Sea. The city was well-known for its university, among other things. Saul may have been named after King Saul, the first king of Israel.

Saul had a physical problem that he called a thorn in the flesh (2 Corinthians 12:17). Historians believe Saul grew up to only be about four and one-half feet tall. Some say he had a balding head with red hair. His thorn in the flesh may have been twisted legs, poor vision, or possibly a posture problem. Whatever his birth defect, Saul did not let his physical problem deter him from getting a good education and pursuing God. He eventually learned to overcome his physical deficiency to serve Christ to the fullest.

Saul went to Jerusalem to study Jewish laws and customs under the renowned scholar Gamaliel. Paul told the high priest in Acts 23:6, "I am a Pharisee, the son of a Pharisee." The Pharisees took pride in observing the Old Testament Law, and they felt they were the authority over all other Jews. The Pharisees dressed to the nines wearing expensive long robes with six inch tassels attached to the hem. They dressed better than the average person, and they were very proud of their outward appearance. They wore little boxes called phylacteries with scriptures inside on their arm or forehead as a further demonstration of their holiness. They placed great emphasis on their outward appearance, but God is more interested in our inward purity and holiness.

Jesus rebuked the Pharisees in Matthew 23. He called them blind guides, hypocrites, and fools. Jesus called them hypocrites seven times in Matthew 23. Jesus complimented them on their beautiful outward appearance, but said they were full of dead men's bones and were unclean as if they were physically dead (Matthew 23:27).

God calls all His children to inward holiness. We are urged to present our bodies a living sacrifice, holy and acceptable to God, which is our reasonable service. We are not to be conformed to this world, but transformed by the renewing of our mind so we are living proof as we reflect the good and perfect will of

God (Romans 12:1-2). We are to slay our personal desires so we can be acceptable in God's sight. The Scriptures call this our reasonable service. We offer self as a living sacrifice in honor of the sacrifice Christ made for us on the cross when He died to cleanse us from all sin.

Saul, the Persecutor

Stephen was a follower of Christ and a deacon in the early church where he became a strong and powerful preacher. Acts 7 gives the account of Stephen appearing before the high priest. He was emboldened to tell the high priest how God had protected and guided great Jewish leaders such as Abraham, Joseph, and Moses through many hardships. Stephen pointed out how the Jews mistreated their fellow man. The Jews did not like his rebuke, so they decided to kill him; but Stephen stood strong in the face of death. The Jews were cut to the heart when Stephen told them they were not keeping the Law by which they judged others (Acts 7:54). They threw Stephen out of the city, stripped him of his clothes, and laid them at young Saul's feet as he watched them stone Stephen to death (Acts 7:58). Stephen asked God to not lay this sin at their feet as he breathed his final breath. Saul obviously felt Stephen's death was justified as he did nothing to stop the stoning.

Saul was a God-fearing man, but he was also a ruthless bounty hunter of Christians. He thought he was doing the right thing by mistreating Christians. In Acts 8:3, Saul made havoc of the church, entering into every house to drag out men and women, sending them to prison because of their faith in Christ.

When we venture out on our own, we too can do things that we feel are right while our actions are counter to what God would have us do. When we don't know Christ or the Holy Spirit, we have no moral compass to keep us on the right path, so we can make the right decisions. Proverbs 16:25 says, "There is a way that seemeth right to a man, but the end thereof are the ways of death."

Saul's Divine Encounter

When Saul matured, he became a devout Pharisee, and he felt his authority over anyone who rebelled against the Old Testament Law. There were many Jews who had converted from Judaism to Christianity. They had dispersed to several other countries in Asia Minor, and Saul felt a strong need to round them up and bring them to Jerusalem for a hearing or trial.

Many early Jewish Christians died because of their faith in Jesus. The chief priest approved Saul going after these wayward Jews who had accepted Christ as their Lord.

In Acts 9:1-2, Saul went to the high priest to obtain a letter of approval to go to Damascus, Syria to bind and bring Christians to Jerusalem. After obtaining the approval of the high priest, Saul headed out to round up Christians. Saul and his traveling companions were nearing the city of Damascus when a very strange thing happened as recorded in Acts 9:3-19. A powerful light shined from heaven on Saul and his posse, and Saul fell blinded to the earth. A loud voice from heaven asked, "Saul, Saul, why persecutest thou me?" Saul asked the voice, "Who art thou, Lord?" Jesus responded, "I am Jesus whom thou persecutest: it is hard for thee to kick against the pricks (*a sharp stick to drive animals)."* Jesus told Saul to go into the city and await instructions on what he should do. Although Saul had not yet accepted Christ, he called Him Lord when he was blinded. God got Saul's full attention.

Saul's companions took him into the city and he fasted without food or drink for three days. In Acts 9:10-19, we are given the account of how Saul was healed both physically and spiritually. Ananias, a disciple and Christian, lived in Damascus. The Lord told Ananias to go to Saul and lay his hands on him so he could receive his sight. Ananias didn't want to go to Saul because he knew how he persecuted Christians. The Lord told Ananias to go to Saul for he was a chosen vessel and would bear Jesus' name to the Gentiles, kings, and children of Israel. Saul was appointed as an apostle before he even believed in Christ. When Ananias got to the house where Saul was staying, he found Saul praying. While Saul prayed, he saw a vision of a man named Ananias laying his hands on him so he could receive his sight. The Holy Spirit was at work in Saul as he confronted his sins.

Jesus would show Saul how severely he would suffer for Christ as he witnessed to others. He would become an instrument in God's hands to lead many to Christ. He would preach Christ to all who would listen including the Jews, Gentiles, kings, and all the Jewish descendants of Israel. He would suffer greatly as a minister of the Gospel just as the Christians who had suffered at his hands before he met the Lord. Saul was to make a drastic change from being a persecutor of Christians to a preacher trying to win more precious souls to Christ. He would pay the high price of following and obeying Christ.

Against his better judgment, Ananias obeyed the Lord and went to see Saul. He called him Brother Saul and told him he had been sent by the Lord to lay his hands on him so his sight could be restored. When this happened, he would also receive the Holy Spirit that had never dwelt in his heart. The scales that covered Saul's eyes fell off and he received his sight. He was baptized immediately and ate some food for the first time in three days.

He stayed with the disciples in Damascus for a few days. Then he started preaching in the synagogues proclaiming Jesus as the Son of God (Acts 9:17-20). Saul had a new message of forgiveness and hope that he was eager to share with others.

The people who had known Saul were amazed at the instant change that had occurred in his life. They knew how he had harassed and abused Christians; and he was now preaching about the redeeming love of Christ. This shows the power of Christ to transform sinful and evil lives into a devoted life of service that can influence others to also make drastic changes for Christ. The Lord can make something beautiful from a sin-soiled life.

The more Saul preached, the more he gained confidence in winning others to Christ. His teaching about Christ confounded and confused the Jews in Damascus as he presented evidence that Jesus is the Messiah. His teaching upset some of the Jews and they conspired to kill him. They sealed the gates to the city so he couldn't escape. Saul's companions lowered him in a basket outside the city walls so he could escape (Acts 9:23-25).

In Acts 9:26-29, Saul did not get a warm welcome by the Christians when he first returned to Jerusalem. They were afraid to associate with him as they had doubts about his conversion in Damascus. Saul then went to Jesus' disciples and they accepted him. He continued preaching freely in Jerusalem but finally returned to his home town of Tarsus after others sought to kill him.

<u>Antioch (Syria)</u>

In Acts 11:19-30, we have the record of Barnabas and Saul in Antioch. After Stephen was stoned to death, ministers dispersed to Phoenicia, Cyprus, and Antioch to preach the message of Christ to the Jews. Many believed on Jesus as the Son of God and turned to Him. The church in

Jerusalem heard what was happening abroad so they sent Barnabas to Antioch so he could return and give them a report on the church. Barnabas saw how the Lord was at work in Antioch as many believed on Christ. He encouraged the new believers to continue their journey and work for the Lord. Barnabas then went back to Tarsus to get Saul to come with him to Antioch. Saul and Barnabas stayed in Antioch for a year as they met with the church and taught many about Christ. The disciples of the early church were first called Christians in Antioch.

Prophets (*inspired teachers and interpreters of God's will*) came from Jerusalem to Antioch to witness the good things happening for the Lord. Agabus, one of the prophets, revealed how a great famine would soon occur in Israel. The Antioch Christians

raised relief money for Israel and sent
it to Judea by Barnabas and Saul.

Chapter Two

Paul's First Mission Trip

In Acts 13:1-3, Barnabas and Saul were commissioned to leave Antioch to go to other countries to preach the good news of the Gospel (*Christ's birth, death, resurrection, and ascension*). Four prophets fasted, prayed, and laid their hands on Barnabas and Saul as they ordained them as missionaries. They were obviously in the will of God as the Holy Spirit spoke to them to send Barnabas and Saul to do the work God intended.

Acts 13:4-41 records their time of ministry on the island of Cyprus. Barnabas, Saul, and their assistant, John Mark, sailed from Tarsus to Cyprus off the coast of Turkey across the Mediterranean Sea. They preached first in the Jewish synagogues located in the coastal town of Salamis. Then they went across the island of Cyprus to Paphos where they encountered a sorcerer (*wizard*) and a false prophet named Bar-Jesus (*Elymas*). He knew the pro-consul, Sergius Paulus, a very intelligent and sensible man. A pro-consul was the governor or military commander of a Roman province. Sergius Paulus called for Barnabas and Saul to visit him so he could hear the Word of God concerning salvation through Christ. Elymas tried to block Barnabas and Saul from meeting with Sergius Paulus as he feared the pro-consul would accept Christ. The devil was working through Elymas to block the salvation message.

Acts 13:9 is the first time Saul is called Paul in the book of Acts, and he is referred to as Paul for the remainder of the book. Paul was filled with the Holy Spirit and he looked sternly in the eyes of Elymas to rebuke him. Paul called Elymas the son of the devil and said he was the enemy of all righteousness. Paul asked him if he would never stop perverting the ways of the Lord.

The devil and his angels work through false teachers to blur the eyes of those who seek Christ. Paul told Elymas he would be blinded by the hand of the Lord, and a mist and darkness fell upon him. Sergius Paulus witnessed what had happened to Elymas and he was amazed at how God worked through Paul to rebuke the false teacher. He was deeply touched by Paul's teaching about Christ, and he accepted the Lord that day.

Perga (*Turkey*)

In Acts 13:13-41, Paul and his companions left Cyprus and sailed to

Perga in Pamphylia where John Mark left them and went back to his home in Jerusalem. Paul did not like John Mark's decision to desert them in the early stages of their first mission trip. Some believe there was a disagreement when Paul and Barnabas started preaching the message of salvation to the Gentiles. It is difficult to overcome a bias or prejudice, and this could have been John Mark's problem. He may have felt strongly the Gospel should only be preached to the Jews, but Jesus had told Ananias before Saul's conversion he would preach to Gentiles and other unbelievers.

Jesus' command to the apostles was to preach, teach, and baptize in all nations including Samaria. This includes every race regardless of their national origin. Sometimes we must lay our preconceived ideas aside to do the work of the Lord. We are not to withhold the Gospel from any group of people as Christ came to save all who will accept Him as Lord.

Paul and Barnabas then left Perga for Antioch in Pisidia in northern Turkey (Acts 13:14). This is not the same Antioch where they were previously before sailing to Cyprus. They sat down with the other worshipers in the synagogue on the Sabbath day. The worship leaders read the Law and then asked Paul and Barnabas if they had any words of encouragement for the people. Paul stood and told them it was God who increased the Jewish population tremendously while their forefathers were slaves in Egypt for over four hundred years. It was God who led them out of slavery and then cared for them while they were in the desert for forty years. God and Moses patiently put up with their grumbling and complaining as they wandered in the desert like Nomads.

God is our example for patience and longsuffering. God intentionally took about four hundred and fifty years from the time the Israelites were first enslaved to the time He eventually gave them the Promised Land in Canaan. He used their trials to strengthen their faith while He delivered and provided their every need daily.

God then gave them judges until the prophet Samuel arrived. The people asked for a king and God gave them King Saul who ruled over them for forty years. God then allowed David to become the king. God loved David dearly and called him a man after His own heart (Acts 13:22).

God then sent His Son Jesus from heaven to earth to be our Savior just as He promised. Paul reminded the descendants of Abraham (*the Jews*) that God had sent His message of salvation to them through Jesus Christ. Paul said the Jews who ruled in Jerusalem rejected, condemned, and killed the Messiah as prophesied in the Scriptures. He told them how Pilate had ignored Jesus' innocence and sentenced Him to die on the cross. Pilate knew Jesus was innocent, but the angry mob ignored the facts and insisted He be crucified. Paul was drawing too many Jews away from Judaism to Christ through His message of grace and mercy, and this was unacceptable to the scribes, Pharisees, and chief priest.

Then Paul taught them the good news of Jesus' resurrection when God raised Him from death. Paul brought to them the good news of how God had kept His promise to their forefathers to raise Jesus from the dead on the third day after He was crucified. Paul quoted Psalm 2:7, "Thou art My Son; this day I have begotten Thee." Jesus will never see the corruption of death again.

David, their forefather, fell asleep in earthly death and was buried with their forefathers. David experienced the corruption of death, but Jesus whom God raised will never die again. He is alive and will live forever as He was raised incorruptible (*flesh that cannot decay in death*)! Paul preached to the Jews the forgiveness of sin through Jesus Christ. He told them they could not be justified (*vindicated, made blameless*) by the Law of Moses, but they could find justification by accepting Christ and obeying His commands. Paul taught the Jews the plain message of salvation so they could clearly see Christ. Paul's desire was that they accept Jesus as their Lord.

Problems in Antioch

The Jews liked what they heard from Paul in the synagogue and begged him to speak again the next Sabbath. They had just gotten a taste of the Gospel and they wanted to hear more. Many of the Jewish Christian converts followed Paul and Barnabas after hearing them speak in the synagogue. The missionaries encouraged the Jews to stand fast in the grace of God. Word spread by word-of-mouth as the Jews told about the message they had just heard from Paul.

The next Sabbath, the synagogue was packed with Jews who had come from across the city of Antioch. They wanted to hear Paul's message of salvation through Christ. The Jewish worship leaders saw what was happening and jealousy took over. They spoke disparagingly about what

Paul told the crowd. The leaders verbally abused Paul and even slandered him (Acts 13:45). Paul and Barnabas boldly told the Jews that they had spoken God's salvation to them first just as God had instructed. These men were fellow Jews of Jesus, and God wanted the Jews to hear the good news of His Son's birth, death, and resurrection first. Some of the Jews rejected the message, so Paul told them in Acts 13:46 they had passed judgment on themselves and had made themselves unworthy of eternal life. Paul and Barnabas would now take the Gospel to the Gentiles (Acts 13:46).

The Lord had instructed Paul and Barnabas to be a light to all the Gentiles in the known world so they could find salvation. Many Gentiles gladly received the truth of the Gospel and received Jesus as their

Lord. They found eternal life when they accepted Christ, and they were ecstatic. The good news of the Gospel spread like wild fire throughout the entire region around Antioch.

The Jews did not like what they were seeing. They got the devout Jewish women of high rank and the leading men in Antioch riled up and they developed a persecution plan for Paul and Barnabas. The leaders then expelled the two missionaries from the region where Antioch was located. Paul and Barnabas were learning about the joy of suffering for Christ's sake. The missionaries responded by shaking the dust of Antioch from their feet as they left for Iconium. Their souls were constantly filled with joy from the Holy Spirit.

Problems in Iconium (Turkey)

Paul and Barnabas left their problems behind in Antioch to go to

Iconium only to find more opposition to their Gospel message. Iconium was known for their many orchards and the wool industry. When they spoke to a large crowd in the synagogue many Jews and Gentiles believed and accepted Christ. The unbelieving Jews stirred up the Gentiles and poisoned their minds against Paul and Barnabas (Acts 14:2). They stayed in Iconium for a long time so they could continue encouraging the new believers. They performed signs and wonders to confirm the truth of their God-given message.

The population of the city was divided: part sided with the Jews, and part with the missionaries. The Jewish and Gentile unbelievers agreed to abusing and the stoning of Paul and Barnabas. When they heard their lives were in danger, they fled to Lystra and Derbe, further east in Turkey. Paul and Barnabas weren't breaking any laws but were just preaching the message of a risen Savior who brings salvation to all who will believe in Him.

Teaching Opportunity in Lystra (*Turkey*)

God opened a door of opportunity for Paul and Barnabas in Lystra, a very small Roman colony. There apparently was no Jewish synagogue in Lystra, so Paul preached outdoors. They met a crippled man who had not been able to walk since birth. The crippled man listened intently as Paul spoke. Paul looked at him compassionately and concluded the man had a strong enough faith to be healed. Paul shouted at the man to stand up, and he did; he leaped up and miraculously walked (Acts 14:10). The witnesses to this man's healing said the gods had come down to them in human form. They called Paul and Barnabas by Greek mythical god's names. The priest of Zeus wanted to join the people in offering garlands and sacrifices of bulls to Barnabas.

The missionaries heard what the people planned, so they became distraught and shouted to the crowd asking what they were doing. Paul and Barnabas told them they were human beings just like them, and they were simply bringing the good news of the Gospel to them. The missionaries had difficulty stopping the people from worshiping them as they still wanted to offer sacrifices. Some troublemakers came from Antioch and Iconium to incite the people even more against Paul and Barnabas. They stoned Paul and drug him out of the city as if he were dead (Acts 14:19). Some of the believers formed a circle around Paul so he could sneak back into town. The next day Paul and Barnabas went to Derbe.

Encouragement in Derbe (Turkey)

Paul and Barnabas preached the Gospel to the people in Derbe and made many disciples. Then they decided to return to some of the cities where they had already preached. They went back to Lystra, Iconium, and Antioch even though they had been persecuted in those places earlier. The missionaries felt a need to go back to encourage and urge the new converts to continue in the faith. The missionaries told them: "We must, through tribulation, enter into the kingdom of God" (Acts 14:22). They appointed elders in each church, fasted, prayed, and ordained the elders for their leadership role.

They visited several other cities where they previously preached, before boarding a ship to sail back to Antioch, the starting point of their first mission trip. They were satisfied they had done the work of the Lord as they had been instructed. This was the shortest of Paul's three mission trips. When they got back home, they called the church members at Antioch together so they could update them on the results of their preaching mission. One of the high lights of the trip was how the door had been opened to preach the Gospel to the Gentiles. They remained with the church in Antioch for some time.

Chapter Three

Paul's Second Mission Trip

The Jews were rightfully proud of the fact God called them His chosen people; but they weren't the only people God loved. The Jews considered the Gentiles as heathen pagans, but God would ultimately give them the same opportunity as He gave the Jews to accept Christ as their Lord.

A dispute surfaced in Acts 15 because the Law of Moses required all Jewish males to be circumcised. This Jewish religious ritual was important and it was passed from one generation of Jews to the next. In Genesis 17, God made a covenant with Abraham that he would have many descendants. God told Abraham to seal the covenant by circumcising every male Jewish baby eight days after birth. Circumcision was required for male babies to be included in the Jewish faith. The Jews tried to impose circumcision on Gentile converts to Christ; but Paul and Barnabas took issue with the Jews as they said it wasn't necessary for male Gentiles to be circumcised so they could be saved (Acts 15:2).

Circumcision was never intended by God as a requirement for salvation. The Jews overlooked the fact that Jesus said He came to fulfil the Law of Moses because of His mercy and grace which superseded the Law. Christians still observe the Law (i.e. The Ten Commandments) because they are a part of our faith foundation; but the Law merges into the grace and mercy of God. It's like a two-lane road merging into an Interstate highway; the two-lane roads did not shut down when the interstate system was built. The interstate system became a better roadway, just as God's law of grace and mercy is a better way than the Mosaic Law.

The Jews who disagreed with Paul and Barnabas decided the two of them should take the dispute over circumcision of the Gentiles to Jerusalem for a final decision. As they passed through the towns and villages on their way to Jerusalem, they didn't miss an opportunity to witness for Christ. The people were filled with joy when they heard about how the Gospel had been preached to the Gentiles and many had accepted Christ.

Paul and Barnabas met with more opposition from the Jews when they arrived in Jerusalem. Some of the Pharisees insisted the male Gentiles must obey the Law and be circumcised if they wanted to be saved. The Jews wanted to change God's truth to bring it into compliance with the Law; but Jesus came to bring the Law into compliance with His mercy and grace.

The council that governed the church listened to the debate. In Acts 15:7-11, Peter stood before the council and boldly proclaimed that God makes no distinction between the Jews and Gentiles. Instead of circumcision, God had purified and circumcised the hearts of the Gentiles by faith. Peter said it was very unfair to put the yoke of the Law on the Gentiles. He reminded the Jews they had a problem with the burden of the Law which they themselves could not keep.

John 1:17 says, "For the law was given by Moses, but grace and truth came by Jesus Christ." Jesus fulfilled the Law through His grace. They testified how God had worked through their ministry to the Gentiles (Acts 15:12). He had empowered them to even perform miracles so the Gentiles would know assuredly they witnessed God's power that had been imparted to Paul and Barnabas.

In Acts 15:13-21, James spoke to the council to support what Paul and Barnabas had said. He quoted from Isaiah 11:10 and Isaiah 54:1-5 where the prophet said God would rebuild the tabernacle of David and raise it up from its ruin. Then the rest of mankind, including the Gentiles, can seek the Lord. James said they should not trouble the Gentiles who were turning to Christ. Instead, James said the Gentiles should be encouraged to abstain from things polluted by idols such as the meat offered on the sacrificial altar. They needed encouragement to avoid sexual immorality, from things strangled, and from blood.

The council in Jerusalem wrote a letter of encouragement to the church in Antioch (Acts 15:23-31). The council was led by the Holy Spirit to not lay the burden of the Jewish Law on the Gentiles. This letter encouraged them to live clean, moral lives before God. The council and the entire church felt they should send Paul, Barnabas, Judas (*Barsabas*), and Silas from Jerusalem to Antioch to settle the dispute over circumcision with the church there. The Christians in Antioch needed to know the church fathers in Jerusalem did not require Gentile males to be circumcised so they could be saved. The Christians in Antioch were elated and they rejoiced when the letter from the council was read. Paul, Barnabas, and Silas stayed for some time in Antioch to preach the Word of God.

Paul and his close associates were human beings with their strengths and weaknesses. They were God-fearing, but they weren't perfect men because of human frailty. Paul told Barnabas he felt they should revisit the churches where they had already preached and see how they were doing. Barnabas agreed but insisted they take John Mark along. Paul strongly disagreed because John Mark had deserted them and went back home prematurely during their first mission trip to Cyprus and Turkey. In Paul's eyes, John Mark had let them and the Lord down, so Paul took a firm stand.

The disagreement between Paul and Barnabas intensified, so the two of them decided to go separate ways. Paul took Silas as his ministry partner and Barnabas took John Mark. Paul wanted someone who would make a commitment to ministry and stick with it regardless of the hardships that would definitely arise. Barnabas and John Mark sailed for Cyprus while Paul and Silas departed for Syria and Cilicia to strengthen the churches.

<u>Calling Timothy</u>

In Acts 16, Paul and Silas arrived in Derbe and Lystra where Paul had previously visited and ministered. A young man by the name of Timothy met Paul and Silas, and they were impressed with him. He had a good reputation according to the local church leaders. Paul decided to take a chance and let Timothy go with them on their journey. The churches there were growing in their faith and in number every day. Young Timothy would learn much from Paul.

Philippi (*Macedonia*) [Acts 16]

A strange thing happened when the trio got to the region of Galatia. They were forbidden by the Holy Spirit to preach the word in Asia (Acts 16:6). They tried to go into Bithynia, but the Spirit did not permit them. The missionaries listened to the Holy Spirit and changed their plans. Notice how God can re-direct our life to fulfil His mission. The three men sailed to Troas where Paul had a vision in the night. In his vision, Paul saw a man from Macedonia pleading for them to come and help them. Paul felt a strong need to follow his dream and go to Macedonia and preach to the people.

On the Sabbath day, the men went to the river where people commonly met to pray. The missionaries met some women on the river bank where Lydia, a God-fearing woman, and other women met. Lydia's heart was opened to what Paul spoke and she decided to be baptized along with other family members that very day.

Some Roman men in the area owned a slave girl who was controlled by an evil spirit. The owners claimed she could foretell future events, so they made considerable money from this demon-possessed slave who was like a fortune teller. The girl followed Paul and the others for several days as she shouted that these men were servants of God, and they could show people the way to salvation. Paul finally got worn out with her constant shouting, so he commanded the evil spirit to come out of her immediately. She was instantly freed from the devil's control. Her owners did not appreciate what Paul had done. They could not profit from this slave as she could no longer be a fortuneteller. They seized Paul and Silas and dragged them before the magistrates for a trial. They stripped their clothes from them and beat them repeatedly. Paul and Silas were thrown into the inner prison where their feet were locked in stocks.

Paul knew how to make the best of a bad situation. Paul and Silas could have had a pity party over the pain on their lacerated backs and the uncomfortable position of having their feet locked in stocks. At midnight, they started singing and praising God while the other prisoners listened. Suddenly there was an earthquake. All the cell doors sprang open and the prisoner's shackles were released. The jailer had been given strict orders to hold Paul and Silas securely. Not only was the jailer's job on the line but he could be put to death if he let his inmates escape. The jailer jumped out of bed and saw the cell doors standing open. He was ready to kill himself with his sword, but Paul told him to not harm himself as all the prisoners were still there.

The jailer came trembling and fell down at the feet of Paul and Silas. He asked them what he must do to be saved and they told him to believe in the Lord Jesus Christ and he would be saved. Paul and Silas taught the jailer and his family about salvation and the entire family was baptized into Christ that night. The jailer cleaned their wounds where they had been beaten and gave them food.

The next day, word from the Roman magistrates came to the jailer to release Paul and Silas. Paul had a stubborn streak, so he told the jailer they would not leave unless the magistrates personally came to apologize for mistreating them, and then lead them out of jail. The magistrates had learned Paul and Silas were Roman citizens so they feared because of the way they had mistreated their fellow citizens. They came to the jail, apologized, and asked them to leave the city, so Paul and Silas left the jail.

A bad situation had a very happy ending as the jailer and his family had all come to Christ because of the unjust suffering of Paul and Silas. The missionaries did not deserve the beating or having their feet locked in stocks. Jesus had said when Saul was first converted in Damascus that he would suffer severely for His sake. Christ had kept His word, but he stood by them while they suffered. Christ knew first-hand about unjust suffering as the Roman soldiers beat and nailed Him to a cross to die for our sins. We too may face suffering for Christ's sake, so be brave and persevere.

Thessalonica (*Macedonia*)

Acts 17 tells about Paul, Silas, and Timothy arriving in Thessalonica. Paul had been concerned about this young congregation. It pleased him to find the church had thrived and grown in spite of suffering and persecution. There was a Jewish synagogue in Thessalonica since there was a large Jewish population in the city. Paul taught in the synagogue on three Sabbath days as he reasoned and debated from the Scriptures.

He told them about Jesus' suffering and His glorious resurrection on the third day after His crucifixion. He proclaimed Christ as the Messiah. Many Greeks and leading women believed Paul's message, but the unbelievers were very upset. The unbelievers formed a mob of rebel-rousers to seize Paul and Silas so they could be punished for preaching such nonsense about Christ. The entire town was in an uproar, so Paul and Silas sneaked out of town during the night to escape punishment.

Berea *(Macedonia)*

Paul and Silas would leave one controversy only to go into another bad situation. They arrived in Berea and were warmly received by the Jews in the synagogue. They eagerly studied the Scriptures to prove what Paul was teaching. As a result, many believed the truth of the Scriptures. They could see Paul was feeding them the truth about Christ, the risen Savior. The troublemakers in Thessalonica heard about what was happening in Berea so they came to stir up the people. The Bereans rushed Paul to the port where he boarded a ship that was bound for

Athens. Silas and Timothy stayed in Berea for only a short time.

Athens (*Greece*)

Paul sent word to Silas and Timothy to leave Berea and join him in Athens. Paul was troubled when he saw the widespread idol worship taking place in Athens. Paul reasoned daily with the Jews and Gentiles in the synagogue and marketplace about their idol worship. Athens was the home of great philosophers like Plato, Aristotle, and Socrates. There were many pagan temples in Athens that added to the problem of idol worship. Some philosophers called Paul a babbler while others said he spoke of a foreign god when he proclaimed Christ and His resurrection.

Paul told them publicly in Acts 17:22-32, "Ye men of Athens, I perceive that in all things you are too superstitious; for as I was passed by and beheld your devotions, I found an altar with this inscription: TO THE UNKNOWN GOD." He accused them of worshipping a god even though they did not know who it was. Paul said the real God does not dwell in temples made with hands, since He gives all breath and life. He made all nations and established their boundaries. God wants us to seek and find Him because He is near to every person. He is a reachable God who stands ready to be a part of our life if we will just accept Jesus as our Lord.

We are God's offspring and in Him all our needs are met. The divine nature of God is not like anything made by man's hands. Paul told them in Acts 17:30, "And the times of this ignorance God winked at (*overlooked*), but now commandeth all men everywhere to repent." Paul reminded the Athenians judgment day is coming when all people will be judged for the deeds they have done on earth. He closed his message by telling them how Jesus was resurrected. His resurrection confirms the appointed Day of Judgment. Only some believed Paul.

Corinth (Greece)

Corinth was the largest city in Greece in Paul's day. Corinth was a bustling city as it was the major east-west thoroughfare for trade. They had two ports where ships discharged their goods and loaded exports from Greece. Corinth is like other major cities with its share of evil and corruption. Immorality and idolatry ran rampant through the city. Sin permeated the population and there seemed to be no escape from all the evil. To put it mildly, Corinth had plenty of challenges on upright moral

living and religious practices. The
church was filled with people
practicing all manner of sins. Paul
and Silas were going to wade into this
cesspool to try and make a difference
for the Lord.

Claudius ruled the Roman Empire,
and he ordered all Jews out of Italy.
Aquila and his wife Priscilla were
Jewish Christians who partnered
with Paul in his ministry (Romans
16:3). They left Italy and came to
Corinth. Aquila, Priscilla, and Paul
had more than ministry in common,
for they all were tentmakers. Paul
made tents so he could have an
income and not burden new
churches with a salary requirement.

Every Sabbath, Paul went to the
synagogue to encourage and
persuade Jews and Gentiles to
accept Christ as their Lord. Some
Jews opposed and rejected Paul's

message about Christ, so he told them he would go to the Gentiles to preach and teach. Crispus, the ruler of the synagogue, and his family believed on the Lord and were baptized along with many other Corinthians.

During the night, Paul had a vision from the Lord who told him in Acts 18:9-10, "Do not be afraid, but speak, and hold not thy peace; for I am with thee, and no man shall set on thee to hurt thee: for I have much people in this city." Crispus would not rule on their complaint against Paul if they were accusing him on matters of the law. Paul stayed in Corinth for eighteen months teaching the Word of God to all who would listen.

Chapter Four

Paul's Third Mission Trip

<u>Ephesus *(Turkey)*</u>

Paul, Aquila, and Priscilla sailed from Corinth to Ephesus where all three of them left the ship. Paul went to the synagogue to teach, but soon afterwards he left to return to Antioch in Syria. He was working his way back to Jerusalem where he would celebrate one of the six annual Jewish feasts.

There was a cultured and eloquent man by the name of Apollos who had come from Egypt to Ephesus. He knew the Scriptures well as he had received some instruction about the Lord. He was a motivated teacher, but he only knew about the baptism for repentance taught by John the Baptist. He had not yet learned about baptism for the remission of sin and the gift of the Holy Spirit we receive at baptism (Acts 2:38). Aquila and Priscilla heard Apollos speak in the synagogue, as he taught them in-depth things he had learned about the Lord. Then Apollos left Ephesus to travel across Greece to teach and encourage those who believed in Jesus. He presented evidence publicly to the unbelieving Jews about the existence of Christ.

Paul witnessed to a group of about twelve disciples and he asked them into what baptism they had been baptized (Acts 19:3). They said they had received John the Baptist's baptism of repentance. Paul taught them about baptism for the remission of sin and the gift of the Holy Spirit, and that day many were baptized in the name of the Lord Jesus. Paul laid his hands on them and the Holy Spirit came on them;

they then spoke in foreign languages (*tongues*) and prophesied.

For the next three months, Paul lectured in the synagogue, persuading, arguing, and pleading the cause of Christ. He got kicked out of the synagogue so he continued teaching five hours every day in the lecture room of Tyrannus. Paul continued teaching for the next two years until all the residents of the region had heard the Word of the Lord regarding salvation. God empowered Paul to perform many miracles to underpin his teaching from the Scriptures. Many were blessed through Paul's teachings about Jesus. They knew Paul had been sent to them by God.

The longer Paul taught, the more opposition he encountered. There was a silversmith named Demetrius who made silver idol shrines to honor the mythical goddess Diana. Demetrius and his fellow craftsmen had a thriving business until Paul came along and taught the people they should serve a living God, not a dead one represented by a piece of silver. Paul's teachings were costing the silversmiths money they needed for their livelihood. Many believers had abandoned idol worship after accepting Christ as Lord. Another concern of the silversmiths was that the temple where idols were worshipped would be weakened. The silversmiths were also trying to protect the glowing image of Diana that would be diminished throughout Asia.

The craftsmen started railing and shouting about Paul and his teaching. They got a horde of people in Ephesus riled up like an angry mob. They drug a couple of Paul's assistants into the amphitheater.

Paul's friends kept him out of this angry mob as they knew the danger he faced. The town clerk was finally able to bring order to the mob. He told them to calm down as everyone knew Ephesus was the home to the guardian of the temple, and Diana's fame would remain. He told them if they had a grievance against Paul to take it to court. Their rioting could not be justified as no one had broken the law.

Greece

Paul embraced his friends in Ephesus, said goodbye, and sailed for Greece where he stayed for three months. Seven of Paul's assistants went ahead of him where they waited for Paul to arrive in Troas where they stayed for one week. On the first day of the week (*Sunday*), the disciples met to break bread before Paul departed on Monday. Paul spoke to them until midnight in the upper room that was lit with many lamps. A young man (*Eutychus*) sat in the window of the upper room and he went into a deep sleep. He fell to the ground from the third floor window and they thought he was dead. Paul went to Eutychus and fell upon and embraced him. He told them he was still alive. Everyone returned to the upper room where Paul taught until daybreak. The young man also came back in and was in good shape, so the people were relieved.

Paul summoned the elders from Ephesus to meet with him before his departure for Jerusalem where he planned to celebrate Passover. Paul told them how he had kept the faith while he served the Lord through tears and trials because of several plots by disbelieving Jews. Paul did not withhold any portion of the Gospel from them as his message was as transparent as crystal. He knew chains and tribulations awaited him in Jerusalem, but this did not cause Paul to avoid going into danger. He said in Acts 20:24, "But none of these things move me, neither count I my life dear unto myself, so that I may finish my course with joy."

Paul was willing to suffer and die if his service to the Lord meant the worst outcome on earth. He had no reason to be ashamed, for he had taught the whole counsel of God wherever he went. Paul told them it was their responsibility to protect the church against false teachers who would come in like hungry wolves. Even men within the church would try and divide the Lord's church that He purchased with His blood.

Paul encouraged the believers to keep the faith so they could receive their final inheritance after this life is over. He told them to take care of the weak so they could receive a giver's blessing from the Lord. Paul knelt and prayed with the men. There was crying and hugging for the men knew this was the last time they would see Paul on earth.

Jerusalem (*Israel*)

After a very sad farewell, Paul tore himself away from the elders at Ephesus and started his long journey on an ocean freighter as he headed toward Jerusalem. He made several stops along the way, changing ships as needed to travel the next leg of his journey. At one stop, he stayed with Philip the evangelist for a few days.

A prophet named Agabus came from Judea to give Paul a very important message. Agabus took Paul's belt and bound himself with it. He told Paul the Jewish leaders in Jerusalem would bind the owner of the belt when he got there, and he would be handed over to the Gentiles (*for punishment*). Paul told them not to weep for he was willing to die in Jerusalem for his Lord. Agabus was willing to take Paul's punishment.

When Paul got to Jerusalem, he was received warmly by his fellow believers. Paul and his associates met with James and the elders to give them a detailed account of all that had happened on their mission trip. The elders were elated that thousands of Jews had believed even though they were zealous of the Old Testament law. The next day Paul went to the temple after going through the usual Jewish custom of purification before entering.

Paul's Arrest

Acts 21:27-36 gives the account of Paul's arrest in Jerusalem. Some

Jews from Asia spotted Paul in the temple so they stirred up the crowd and seized him as if he was a criminal. They said he had preached against the Law and he had polluted the temple by allowing Greeks (*Gentiles*) to enter. The whole city got in an uproar; they apprehended Paul, dragged him out of the temple, and slammed the temple doors shut.

They started beating Paul but the commandant (*centurion*) and soldiers came in to stop them. The commandant then arrested Paul and secured him with two chains. He asked Paul who he was and what he had done. Paul was sent to the barracks so he would be protected from the shouting mob. Paul was so weak from the beating the soldiers had to carry him. The mob that followed kept shouting that they should kill Paul. He asked the commandant if he could stand and address the angry mob.

Paul started speaking boldly in Hebrew to the angry people and the mob listened. He wanted them to relate to him as their fellow Jew. Paul told them he was a Jew and had learned at the feet of Gamaliel in their beloved city of Jerusalem. Gamaliel had taught Paul according to the strictest interpretation of the Mosaic Law the Jews practiced. Paul related how he had harassed Christians with the same zeal they were demonstrating against him. He confessed to even being responsible for the death of men and women who professed faith in Christ.

He told how the high priest and the Sanhedrin council had granted permission for him to hunt down Christians and bring them to Jerusalem for punishment or death.

Paul then testified how he was struck blind by the Lord as he neared Damascus to round up more Christians. He related how God had healed him of blindness when Ananias was sent by the Lord to lay hands on him and pray with him. Paul wanted them to see how badly he had mistreated Christians. In Paul's earlier days he was just as anti-Christian as those who now wanted to punish him.

He testified before the Sanhedrin council how he was baptized after being healed from blindness, and then he became God's mouthpiece to spread the Gospel to all who would believe.

The people listened to Paul, but then they turned on him for all the bad things he had done to Christians. The crowd became unruly so the commandant brought Paul inside the barracks so they could scourge and whip him. They stretched him out with leather strips before they flogged him. Paul asked the commandant if it was legal to flog him since he was a Roman citizen and had not been condemned in a trial. They didn't flog him, but they put Paul back in chains.

In Acts 23, Paul again appeared before the Sanhedrin council. He gazed intently at them and told them how he had lived for and served God faithfully as a devout Jew. The high priest ordered those who stood near Paul to strike him in the mouth. Paul told the high priest he was being judged by the same Law of which they stood in defiance.

The council was made up of Pharisees and Sadducees. The Pharisees believed in the resurrection of the dead, but the

Sadducees did not. Paul took advantage of this difference of opinion between the council members. He told them he was a Pharisee and he was being judged because of his belief in the resurrection. This statement caused an argument within the council. The Pharisees did not find Paul guilty of anything worthy of punishment. The argument accelerated so the commandant told the troops to return Paul to the barracks for his protection.

The Lord stood beside Paul that night and told him to take courage for he had been a faithful witness. Paul had said he would go to Rome and witness to the Christians there regardless of the consequences. The next morning a group of over forty men took an oath they would not eat or drink until they had killed Paul. Paul's nephew learned of the plot to kill his uncle so he went and told the commandant what the mob was planning. The commandant wrote a letter to Felix the governor and told him they would bring Paul to him for a hearing before his accusers. Paul was placed in Herod's castle for protection.

In Acts 24, we are told that five days later the high priest, some elders, and Tertullus a forensic legal advocate came to present their evidence against Paul to the governor. Tertullus stroked Felix's ego by telling him what a great governor he was and how much they appreciated what he had done. He then told Felix how Paul was like a pest and agitator causing a great division among the Jews. He called Paul a ring leader as he created confusion. They asked Felix to interrogate Paul to hear firsthand what a trouble maker he was.

Paul stood before Felix and gladly made a defense for himself. He was relaxed and cheerful as he stood to be questioned. Paul told Felix he had been in Jerusalem for more than twelve days where he worshipped in the temple and synagogue without causing any problems. He neither argued with the Jews nor brought an angry mob with him to create problems. He boldly spoke up for God and Christ in whom he fully believed. He spoke of the hope of the resurrection that he was confident was a gift from God. Paul testified that he had lived a clean, moral life as he sacrificed his lusts, bodily appetites, and worldly desires. His utmost desire was to have a clear and blameless conscience without any offense against the God in whom the Jews believed.

He requested Felix to ask his accusers to present their evidence of any wrong he had committed. He wanted to know if he was being indicted simply because he believed in the resurrection. Felix declined to make a decision and told the centurion to keep Paul in custody, but to give him some liberties. Paul's friends would now be able to visit him to meet his needs.

Several days later, Felix and his wife were together. Felix asked that Paul be brought to tell them more about his faith in Christ. Paul talked about moral purity, controlling human passions, and God's pending judgment. This upset and terrified Felix, so he sent Paul from his presence and told him he would send for him at a more convenient time. It distressed Felix when Paul bluntly spoke the truth of God. Felix left his office as governor after two years. He spoke often with Paul, but when he departed, he left Paul in chains.

Festus became the new governor to replace Felix. Festus went to Jerusalem to meet the high priest and other prominent Jews who urged him to do something about his prisoner Paul. They asked the governor to bring Paul back to Jerusalem. Their secret plan was to ambush and kill Paul. Festus invited the high priest and Jews to send their representatives with him to Caesarea where Paul was imprisoned to bring formal charges against him, so the men went to Caesarea to charge Paul. They brought many false and unprovable accusations against Paul.

Festus wanted to appease the Jews from Jerusalem, so he asked Paul if he was willing to go to Jerusalem to stand trial before the Sanhedrin. Festus was willing to go with him. Paul told Festus he stood as an innocent man for judgment to be rendered in Caesarea, not Jerusalem. Paul said if he deserved to die in Festus' opinion, he was not begging off if he had broken any laws. If Festus could not decide the case, Paul asked for an appeal before Caesar the emperor. Festus did not want to kill him, but he wanted to pass the buck to the Sanhedrin for action.

Several days later, the king came to visit Festus to congratulate him on his new office as governor. Festus told the king about Paul's hearing before him and the witnesses against him from Jerusalem. King Agrippa wanted to hear Paul's testimony, so he and his wife Bernice appeared the next day with great pageantry. They were surrounded by the military leaders and leading citizens of Caesarea in the audience hall.

King Agrippa told Paul in Acts 26:1 he could speak on his own behalf. Paul asked the king to listen to him patiently as he laid out his own defense. He said the Jews who accused him would testify of his youthful days when he studied the Mosaic Law and how he lived as a Pharisee. Paul threw himself at the mercy of the king because of his belief in the resurrection. Paul said he was considered a criminal by the Jews because he believed in the resurrection. He asked the king why they thought it was so incredible that God could bring about resurrection.

Paul related to the king how he, at one time, had punished Christians for their faith, and how he received Christ in Damascus. He said the Lord saved him so he could be His witness to the world. God called him out of Judaism so he could preach the Gospel to the Gentiles. God worked through Paul to open the eyes of Gentiles who needed deliverance from and forgiveness for their sins. Paul had obeyed the call of God.

Paul told the king when he preached repentance to the Gentiles, the Jews seized him in the temple so they could kill him. He told the king it was by the grace of God that he could stand before him to tell about his ministry that was appointed by God. He told the king about how Christ came, suffered, died, and was resurrected. He was only preaching the truth that had been prophesied for centuries by the Old Testament prophets. Festus thought Paul's great learning had made him insane. Paul told the king what he had done in his witnessing was transparent; and nothing was under-handed about his ministry. Paul asked the king if he believed the prophets who were God's messengers. Paul's opinion was that the king believed.

Festus thought Paul was trying to get him to accept Christ. Paul told him his desire was that all who heard his witness that day, including the king, would come to Christ. King Agrippa left the room and told Festus Paul had done nothing to deserve death.

In Acts 27, Paul, Luke, and other prisoners boarded a ship for Italy. Centurions guarded Paul and the other prisoners on their voyage. It was October and the seas were treacherous at that time of year. The ship's pilot had difficulty sailing in the strong winds. Paul feared for their safety and told the centurion guard of his concerns. The guard disregarded what Paul said as he preferred to listen to the pilot and the owner of the ship. They sailed into danger, and a very strong wind similar to a typhoon hit the ship. The pilot stopped navigating and lowered the sails so the ship could drift with the strong winds.

The next day the winds were still very strong, so they threw cargo overboard. On the third day of the storm, they threw the ship's tackle and furniture into the sea. They drifted for several days while the winds continued blowing. Neither the crew nor the two hundred and seventy-six people on board had been able to eat for several days. They didn't eat for fourteen days. On the fourteenth day, they threw the wheat overboard.

At daybreak, the pilot spotted land so he cut the cables to the anchors and plowed the bow of the ship into the sandy beach. The waves started breaking up the ship's stern. The counsel of the soldiers wanted to kill the prisoners so they would not escape, but the centurion guarding Paul did not want him to die. He commanded that all who could swim should do so. Some clung to pieces of wood from the ship that had broken apart.

Acts 28 continues the outcome after they had all reached land. Fortunately, no one had died in the violent storm. The island natives welcomed their visitors who arrived on the island under very adverse circumstances. It was raining a cold winter rain so they gathered sticks to build a fire. A small poisonous viper came out of the sticks and bit Paul on the hand when he placed the sticks on the fire. Paul shook the small snake from his hand into the fire and the bite did him no harm. When Paul did not swell or die, the natives concluded he was a god.

Publius, the island chief who owned estates on the island, welcomed and entertained the survivors for three days. The father of Publius was very sick in bed with a high fever and dysentery. Paul prayed for him and laid his hands on him, and the man was healed. The other ailing people on the island came to Paul, and they too were healed. Three months later, the people of the island stocked their next ship with all the provisions they needed before sailing to Syracuse.

They finally reached Rome after making several stops. The prisoners were delivered to the captain of the guard, but Paul was allowed to live alone with his guard. Paul wanted to relate to the officials why he came in chains to Rome. He told all that had happened to him in Jerusalem and Caesarea, and how false charges that would not hold up in a court of law had been lodged against him. He witnessed to them about Christ in Acts 28, and as usual, some believed while others did not. This caused confusion and disagreement because he spoke of the resurrection.

Paul was finally freed as a prisoner. He rented a house and stayed in Rome two years. He received many visitors to whom he preached freely and openly about Jesus Christ, and no one harmed or hindered him.

Paul is an inspiration to every child of God. His tenacity in serving God under very adverse circumstances gives us a pattern on how we are to depend on God in all of life's problems, no matter how severe they may be.

Chapter Five

The Price for Preaching

When Saul initially accepted Christ, he made a complete commitment to Him. He was always fully committed at whatever he did. He went all out to persecute Christians before he was converted, and he then went all in for Christ when he decided to do all he could for Christ and His kingdom. Consequently, Paul made many friends and enemies in his ministry. The truth can either offend or draw people to Christ. This was certainly the case with Paul, and it is still true today. Some hear and want to give their lives to Christ, while others want no part of what Jesus offers (*forgiveness of sins and eternal life in a perfect place*).

When we are faced with the decision to accept or reject Christ, some walk away in denial of their need for a Savior. Others see they are lost in sin and have no real purpose in life. There is a natural void in our life without Christ and only He can fill the emptiness and lift the load of guilt. We can try unsuccessfully to fill the spiritual void with earthly things, but the void persists. Jesus came to earth to make us whole in Him. What a kind and compassionate Savior we serve for His blood cleanses us from our sins.

Those who disagreed with Paul's teachings about a risen Savior often took extreme actions to stop his message. The chief priest, Pharisees, and many Jews were concerned that he was preaching a message of God's grace and mercy instead of the Mosaic Law. This caused many conflicts for Paul, but he never wavered in his faith. He was quite content to preach the truth of the gospel even if it meant persecution and death.

Suffering is a part of God's plan for His children. He corrects and chastises us out of love just as a parent disciplines their children. God's punishment is intended to draw us closer to Him as our Creator, Provider, and Heavenly Father. The basis and requirement for suffering is clearly outlined in the New Testament. Jesus told us we will suffer for His sake. Jesus' and Paul's response to suffering is confirmed in several New Testament verses:

- Jesus: Blessed are ye, when men shall revile you, and persecute you, and shall say all manner of evil against you falsely, for my sake (Matthew 5:11).
- Jesus: And ye shall be hated of all men for my name's sake: but

he that endureth to the end
shall be saved (Matthew 10:22).
- Jesus: He that findeth his life
shall lose it: and he that loseth
his life for my sake shall find it
(Matthew 10:39).
- Jesus: For I will shew him how
great things he must suffer for
my name's sake (Acts 9:16).
- Paul: Therefore I take pleasure
in infirmities, in reproaches, in
necessities, in persecutions, in
distresses for Christ's sake: for
when I am weak, then I am
strong (2 Corinthians 12:10).
- Paul: For unto you it is given in
behalf of Christ, not only to
believe on him, but also to
suffer for his sake. (Philippians
1:29).

Suffering is a part of our service to
Christ. We never enjoy suffering from
a human perspective, but it is a
requirement for all Christ-followers.

Consider how He suffered on the cross for us. We may suffer in different ways including rejection, hatred, isolation, verbal abuse, etc. Some unfortunately suffer at the hands of other family members as they want no part of Christ or anyone who has claimed Him as their Savior.

Paul endured much suffering because he preached so strongly about the love and forgiveness of Christ. He told about God's mercy and grace that superseded and fulfilled the Mosaic Law. He taught repentance, confession, and baptism and many gladly received Christ as their Lord. Others made Paul suffer greatly including beatings, threats on his life, and false charges about his faith. He was even called a devil, but Paul never lost faith or hope. He clung to Christ for he knew He would bring him through his problems. Paul understood his earthly problems were a prelude to spending eternity with Christ.

Paul knew why he suffered so much, and he was faithful to the end. History tells us he was finally beheaded in a Roman prison. His suffering should enable us to put our suffering into perspective. Paul encourages us to not be afraid regardless of our circumstances. We have the opportunity to call on God to meet our needs. The Holy Spirit ministers to our needs and sustains us through trials, afflictions, and losses. Keep a strong faith in the Lord and He will see you through.

Part Two

Paul's Letters to the Churches

Chapter Six

Paul the Letter Writer

Paul would go from one city to another to preach the good news of the Gospel about his resurrected Lord. The message gained traction wherever he preached as many believed and accepted Christ. Paul planted and established a new church in many of the cities where he preached, so church families could come together to worship after Paul departed. Elders were appointed as the spiritual over-seers of each congregation. Many churches today follow the same model of elder leadership in local congregations. These men are charged with the responsibility of keeping the church unified through truthful preaching and teaching from the Scriptures. They are also the guardians against false teaching and improper conduct within the church.

Paul used his excellent education when he started writing letters of instruction and encouragement to the churches he had planted. He wrote thirteen or fourteen letters. The author of the book of Hebrews is unknown, but many feel Paul wrote Hebrews due to the writing style he commonly used.

An overview of each of Paul's epistles *(letters)* to eight churches and three individuals who labored with him during his various mission trips will be briefly discussed in this book.

First Corinthians

Paul wrote two letters to the church at Corinth around A.D. 56. First Corinthians was written while Paul was on his third mission trip in Ephesus, and Second Corinthians was written while he was in Philippi that same year.

Paul visited Corinth on his second mission trip and planted a church there. Paul's outward appearance apparently did not leave the best first impression in spite of his superior education. Apollos visited the church in Corinth and many Gentiles fell in love with his appearance and silver-tongued eloquence. Consequently, there was division in the church as its members took sides between Paul and Apollos.

Corinth was a very progressive and liberal city. Worldly practices had invaded the church, and the people were divided on which man to follow. Paul wrote First Corinthians to unify the church and call them out on the sins in the church that needed to be addressed and corrected. He told the members in First Corinthians 1:11-

13 they were divided over Paul, Apollos, Cephas (*Peter*), and Jesus. He asked them if Christ is divided, or if Paul was crucified for them.

They needed to gain spiritual maturity over church leadership and correct their carnal desires. The church is Christ's light of truth that is to shine into a dark world of sin. Unfortunately, there was a sin problem in the church at Corinth, and this dimmed the light of the Gospel. Paul's aim was to get everyone's attention off of a man and their lustful desires so they could focus solely on Christ. He admonished them to live pure lives in a sinful city. Paul wanted the church to be a shining example in a cesspool of sin in their city.

Paul urged the church in Corinth to address and correct some specific sins and problems:

Shun Evil

The church is an extension of what Christ did while He was on earth. He was humble in every respect and had a deep love for those in physical or spiritual need. But the church in Corinth had lost their focus on Christ.

First Corinthians 5:1-13 outlines specific actions for the church to take to purge out sexual immorality that existed. A son had committed fornication with his father's wife. Paul said this is impure and condemned. He told them forthright to expel this person from their church and deliver him to Satan for physical punishment. Paul's desire was that this discipline would draw the young man back to God, for he needed to repent and receive God's forgiveness and restoration.

Some in the church were boastful, and Paul told them this is totally out of place in any church. He urged the leadership to look to Christ who was sacrificed as their Passover Lamb. He called them to purity, sincerity, and the truth. He told them to not associate on a regular basis with sinners including those who were immoral, greedy, cheaters, and idolaters. Furthermore, Paul said there were those who were more devoted to an idol object than to God. There were others in the church that had foul tongues, were drunkards, swindlers, and robbers. The church had plenty of problems and Satan was behind them all.

The church's influence in the community was weakened tremendously due to the sins of its members. The world had invaded the church who is the bride of Christ, and Paul wanted them to make tough decisions to expel the evil doers so the faithful could get back to serving a sinless Savior. Paul knew if they did not correct their problems, the church could not survive because they had lost their focus on Christ.

Legal Actions

In First Corinthians six, Paul told the church it was wrong to take legal action against someone before ungodly men *(in court)* rather than resolving the problem within the church family. He said petty issues should be resolved internally in the church rather than taking legal action. He shamed them and said the church members were capable of settling disputes, private grievances, and quarrels. Some of the judges were Gentile unbelievers so Paul advised them to settle their differences within the family of believers. Paul concluded it is better to suffer loss than alienating themselves through decisions made by unbelievers.

Other Sins

Paul listed other damning sins he had heard about in the church. First Corinthians 6:9-10 lists specific sins including immorality, idolatry, adultery, homosexuality, cheating, greed, drunkenness, foul-mouthed revilers, slanderers, and robbers. Satan was having a hey-day within the church, but Paul tried desperately to get them to forsake sin and turn to God.

We might conclude from this list there are big sins and little sins, but all sin is an abomination or repulsive to God. Jesus told the Pharisees in Luke 16:15, "Ye are they which justify yourselves before men; but God knoweth your hearts; for that which is highly esteemed among men is abomination in the sight of God." God abhors all sin regardless of what we think.

Love is the foundational theme of First Corinthians. Disunity, division, and impurity can be overcome if we love God and our fellow man as we should. We must sacrifice self to be fully used by God. David talked about having clean hands and a pure heart in Psalm 24:4. This is exactly what Paul wanted every member of the Corinthian church to habitually practice. We must rid ourselves of sin to be used by God.

Paul is famous for his explanation of love recorded in First Corinthians chapter thirteen. He outlined what love is and is not; and what love does and does not. The real test of love for any person is found in the first three verses of the chapter. Paul wrote:

- If Paul could speak many languages as an angel and did not have love, his life would be like sounding brass or a tinkling cymbal.
- If Paul had the gift of prophecy, understood all mysteries, had all knowledge like a genius, and had enough faith to move mountains, he would be nothing without love.
- If he gave all he had to feed the poor and gave his body to be burned at the stake, and didn't have love, it would not profit anything.

Then Paul wrote what love does:

- It suffers long (*patience*), and is kind;
- Love rejoices in the truth;
- Love bears up under any trial that comes our way.

- Love has enduring faith, hope, and perseveres all things.

Paul also listed what love is not or does not:

- There is no envy or jealousy in love, it is not boastful, and does not display any sign of egotism;
- It is not conceited or inflated with pride, it is not rude or unmannerly, and does not act in an unbecoming manner, love does not insist on having its own way as it is not self-seeking, love is not touchy or resentful, and it does not keep records of wrong or suffering;
- Love does not rejoice at injustice and unrighteousness;
- Love never fades, fails, or becomes obsolete. True love never ends.

Paul's conclusion on love is recorded in First Corinthians 13:13, "And now abideth faith, hope, charity (*love*), these three; but the greatest of these is charity."

Paul closed the letter of First Corinthians on a very positive note. He had bluntly told the church about their sin problem. He then fed them with a strong discourse on love.

In the fifteenth chapter of First Corinthians he reminded them of the resurrection of Jesus after He was crucified. His resurrection gives us a strong hope of our own bodily resurrection when Jesus returns. Paul was privileged to see Jesus after His resurrection, so he was an eye-witness to the power of God over death. He said if our only hope is restricted to this life, then we are in a pitiful condition.

At the resurrection when Jesus comes back, wonderful things will happen. The saints who died an earthly death will have been asleep in Jesus. When we come forth from our burial place, we will receive a new glorified body just like the glorified body Christ received when he came forth in victory over death. Our bodies are buried in weakness but will rise in power; they are buried in the corruption of decay but will be raised incorruptible; our natural bodies will be raised spiritual bodies.

Second Corinthians

Some of the brethren in the church at Corinth apparently discredited Paul's divine appointment as an apostle, but Paul needed to convince them otherwise. He pointed out his willingness to suffer extremely to serve Christ and preach the good news of the Gospel. In Second Corinthians 11:25-33, Paul said he was beaten with 39 stripes five times by fellow Jews, he was beaten three

times with rods, and was ship-
wrecked three times. They even
stoned Paul once because of his
faith. We can wonder if Paul's
sufferings for Christ brought back
bad memories of how he had
persecuted Christians prior to his
conversion. Paul's faith never
wavered in spite of the hardships he
had to suffer.

Paul told them in Second
Corinthians 1:21, "Now he which
stablished us with you in Christ, and
hath anointed us, is God." Paul was
divinely anointed to preach to the
believers in Corinth and other places.
His ministry had been sealed by God.
The Holy Spirit had been given to him
as God's guarantee and stamp of
approval.

He urged them to be willing to forgive
wrong-doers in the church.
Forgiveness is an absolute necessity

if we are to be made whole. We experience the power of forgiveness of sins when we accept Christ. The forgiven feel the warmth of Christ's love and the cleansing power of His shed blood. Christ told us in His model prayer to forgive others who have wronged us just as Christ forgives. Sin must be forsaken so we can receive forgiveness.

Paul addresses separation from sin in Ephesians 4:21-24. He said we are to put off the old man of sin so we can be a new creation in Christ. The sinful person we were was driven by human lusts and desires, but we put on a new spirit when we accept Christ. The decision starts with the mind and convinces our heart to give up sin for salvation. We dismiss Satan so we can be more like God.

Paul paints a beautiful word picture in Second Corinthians 2:14-16 when he said God leads us to triumph in Christ. He diffuses the fragrance of His knowledge in all places. We become a sweet-smelling fragrance to God, to the saved, and the unsaved. We are an aroma that leads to life eternal. Our Christian influence makes a difference in the world.

We become living letters that are not written with ink on tablets of stone, but spiritual letters written on our heart. Our sufficiency is of God as we witness to others about what Christ has done and is doing in our life. Our ministry of righteousness far exceeds our previous life when we lived for Satan.

When the Jews practiced the Law that was given by God to Moses, the full Gospel was veiled, but when Christ came, He lifted the veil. His grace and mercy shines forth giving us liberty in Christ that the Law could not afford. Disbeliever's eyes are still veiled from the truth of God. The message Paul preached and ministers still preach today, can lift the veil when truth is revealed. The mystery of salvation becomes clear when we hear the truth preached and let the Holy Spirit convict us of sin.

Paul was courageous in the face of persecution and death. He had suffered much so he could preach the good news of Jesus' love, forgiveness, resurrection, and ascension. He testified in Second Corinthians 4:8-9, "We are troubled (*hard-pressed*) on every side, yet not distressed (*crushed*); we are perplexed, but not in despair; persecuted, but not forsaken; cast down, but not destroyed." Paul's hope and trust was firmly planted in Jesus Christ. He realized the suffering we endure in this life is temporary, but our hope is in eternity where there will be no more pain or death. He said our light affliction in this life is but for a moment when compared to eternity. Paul's focus was on the unseen things of glory, not his present problems.

Paul was assured he would eventually receive a glorified body that would never see death. We escape the second death when we accept Christ and commit to living a sacrificial life for Him. Our eternal home in heaven will not pass away like our mortal bodies that must die before we leave this earth. Our mortal life will be swallowed up by eternal life. God has given us the Holy Spirit as our guarantee of eternity.

Paul said in Second Corinthians 5:6, 8, "Therefore we are always confident, knowing that, whilst we are at home in the body, we are absent from the Lord. We are confident, I say, and willing rather to be absent from the body, and to be present with the Lord."

Paul declared in Second Corinthians 6:2, "For he saith, I have heard thee in a time accepted, and in the day of salvation have I succored (helped) thee: behold, now is the accepted time; behold, now is the day of salvation." There should be an urgency to accept Christ while we have the opportunity. The time will come through death when it will be too late to receive Christ as our Lord.

Paul admonished the Christians in Corinth to come back to God by giving up their worldly affections. He told them plainly to not be unequally yoked to unbelievers. We are temples of God; we are admonished to live pure and holy lives. We are to convince unbelievers to accept Christ or separate from them. This seems harsh, but these were the instructions Paul gave the church. They needed to purge sin from their church if they were going to make a difference in Corinth. The change could be through repentance or expulsion. Paul preferred they repent of their sins, but he did not rule out expulsion from the church if members continued in their sins. He told them in Second Corinthians 7:1, "Having therefore these promises, dearly beloved, let us cleanse ourselves from all filthiness of the flesh and spirit, perfecting holiness in the fear of God.

Paul taught the church a lesson on being free-hearted through his own sacrificial giving. In Second Corinthians eight, he talks about God's grace that had been bestowed on the Macedonian churches. They suffered affliction and poverty, but they gave liberally to Paul's ministry. They had first given themselves to Christ, so they wanted to share in Paul's ministry. They knew the blessing of giving, and they demonstrated their faith and love through financial support.

He wrote in Second Corinthians 8:9 that Christ was rich before He came to earth; yet for our sakes He became poor, that we through His poverty could become rich. We have become joint-heirs with Christ to all God's riches.

Paul re-visits the topic of liberal giving in Second Corinthians 9:6-13. He makes several important points about our giving to His kingdom:

- If we give sparingly, we will also reap sparingly;

- If we sow (*give*) bountifully, we will reap bountifully;
- We are to give cheerfully, not out of grudge or necessity;
- We will receive God's abundant blessings for every good work;
- He will increase the seed He has given us to sow, and increase our fruits of righteousness;
- Liberality produces thanksgiving;
- Liberality becomes natural because of our desire to obey.

A right mind will always produce the right results.

Paul wanted to clarify the purpose of his ministry in Second Corinthians ten. He was engaged in warfare with Satan. He encountered disbelief, scorn, threats, and imprisonment. He did not use physical weapons to battle Satan, but he used the Word of God as his sword that could pull down strongholds. The Holy Spirit could help Paul refute arguments and prideful people. Some said Paul's bodily presence was weak, and his speech was contemptible, but his letters were powerful. Paul did not let criticism or opposition deter him from performing his utmost for God.

Paul made a startling statement in Second Corinthians 11:3 when he wrote that he was concerned that Christian's minds can be corrupted by the simplicity that is in Christ. God's plan of salvation is very clear and simple. We need not add to or take away from His plan, as it is sufficient for our salvation.

Paul addressed his physical defect in Second Corinthians 12:7-10. We don't know what Paul's 'thorn in the flesh' was, but he felt it was holding him back from performing to the maximum in his ministry. Paul asked the Lord three times to remove the problem, but Jesus told Paul, "My grace is sufficient for thee; for my strength is made perfect in weakness." Paul felt his problem was given to him lest he be exalted above measure in his ministry. Christ will give us the strength to do His work regardless of our limitations or problems.

Paul closed Second Corinthians with a benediction on behalf of the church he loved. In Second Corinthians 13:11-14 he prayed, "Finally, brethren, farewell. Be perfect, be of good comfort, be of one mind, live in peace; and the God of love and peace shall be with you. Greet one another with an holy kiss. All the saints salute you. The grace of the Lord Jesus Christ, and the love of God, and the communion of the Holy Ghost, be with you all. Amen."

Chapter Seven

The Book of Romans

Paul was most likely in Corinth on his third mission trip when he wrote the book of Romans to the believers in Rome about A. D. 57. He needed to prepare them for his upcoming visit to Rome. His letter was intended to encourage them in their faith, and also establish his divine appointment as an apostle. His letter is a treatise that deals with their faith and the doctrine of salvation that God gave.

Paul was like an attorney who tries to convince the court and jury of the guilt or innocence of the defendant. Paul clearly outlined the need, the method, and the scope of salvation. His argument was simple to understand as it is God's plan of salvation. He presented God's plan with authority, and this lent credibility to Paul's apostleship through his divine appointment.

- The Need for Salvation
  Paul made two very forceful points that show every person is in need of salvation. Romans 3:10, "There is none righteous, no not one." We were each born with a sin nature; therefore, we need a restoration called salvation to establish a relationship with God. Then Paul said in Romans 3:23, "For all have sinned, and come short of the glory of God." It does not matter if a person is a Jew or Gentile; we are all sinners and need salvation. It is only through Christ that we find reconciliation with

God. It is through the shed blood of Christ that our sins are canceled and blotted out; His blood cleanses us from all sin (1 John 1:7).

- The Method of Salvation
    1. Hearing: Romans 10:17 says, "So then faith cometh by hearing, and hearing by the word of God." We must hear and then have faith in God's promise of forgiveness for sin.
    2. Confession: We must confess that Jesus is the risen Son of God. Romans 10:9 says, "That if thou shalt confess with thy mouth the Lord Jesus, and shalt believe in thine heart that God hath raised

him from the dead, thou shalt be saved."

3. <u>Repentance</u> of our sins shows God and man we regret our wrong-doing and want to make things right. Second Peter 3:9 says, "The Lord is not slack *(tardy)* concerning his promise, as some men count slackness; but is longsuffering to us-ward, not willing that any should perish, but that all should come to repentance."

4. <u>Immersion</u> into Christ has a two-fold purpose: 1) for the remission of sins, and 2) to receive the gift of the Holy Spirit (Acts 2:38). Jesus said in Mark 16:16, "He that believeth and is baptized shall be saved;

The Apostle Paul

but he that believeth not shall be damned." Cleansing from sin opens the door for the Holy Spirit to dwell in our hearts to lead and guide us in our daily spiritual journey.

- The Scope of Salvation
  Romans 6:1-14 gives the reasons we are not to continue in sin after we accept Christ as our Lord:
  1. So God can more fully demonstrate His grace. We die to sin when we find new life in Christ Jesus.
  2. We are baptized and buried into Christ's death and are raised like He was when He was resurrected. We are re-born a new creation, so we adopt a new life. Immersion is a

reflection of His death, burial, and resurrection.

3. The old sinful man (*person*) died to sin just as Christ died on the cross. The sinful body is destroyed so we will not serve sin any longer.

4. We die with Christ at baptism so we can also live with him. When Christ received a new glorified body at His resurrection, we too receive a new spiritual body at baptism.

5. We are dead to sin, but we are alive unto God through Jesus Christ our Lord.

6. We are to yield our bodies as instruments of God and His righteousness, for we have been saved by the

grace *(unmerited favor)* of
God.

The result and blessings that come
from salvation are numerous. Our
blessings are recorded in Romans
5:1-11:

- We have peace with God;
- Our patience matures through
  tribulations;
- Hope increases as we lean more
  upon God for His help;
- We know and feel the love of
  God because we are now one of
  His adopted children;
- We know the joy of salvation
  because of Jesus' sacrificial
  death for us.

In Romans five, Paul writes about the
blessings of being justified and made
right with God. He said we have been
justified *(acquitted)* by our faith; we
have made peace with God through
His Son Jesus. Through faith, we

have access to God's grace in which we stand firmly. We should rejoice in the hope we have found in God. Because of Christ's triumph over death, we should rejoice, even when we are having trouble. Hardship produces patience and endurance; endurance matures character; character produces a confident hope of eternal salvation; hope never disappoints because God's love has filled our hearts through the Holy Spirit.

Christ died for us when we needed Him most in our spiritual weakness due to sin. We cannot do anything to earn salvation, but Christ died in our place so we can receive salvation through Him. He died for us when we were afar off because of His genuine sacrificial love. We have received the blessing of reconciliation to God due to Christ's death. We are sinners due to one man's (*Adam's*) sin and we face a death sentence; but we are saved for eternity due to one Man's *(Jesus')* death and resurrection. One man's sin led to condemnation for all men, but another Man's act of righteousness leads to acquittal for all who will receive Christ. Adam disobeyed and sinned, but Christ obeyed and died. Sin reigned in death, but God's grace reigns in righteousness.

We don't continue in sin so God's grace can abound. We died to sin when we came to Christ. When we are baptized, we are baptized into His death. Jesus came forth with a new glorified body when He was resurrected, and in His likeness we arise from baptism a new creation in Him. We are like Christ in His death and resurrection. The sinful person was crucified when we abandoned sin, so we are freed from sin. We die with Christ, so we will live with Him.

Paul warns us to not let sin be a part of our life moving forward. We are to present ourselves to God as being alive from death. Sin no longer rules our lives as we depend on the Holy Spirit to guide us in all things. We have changed from slaves of sin to servants for Christ.

We have been set free from the Law and sin so we can serve Christ freely. God condemned sins of the flesh when He sent Christ to earth to ransom us from sin. He paid our sin debt when He shed His blood on the cross. We now think spiritual instead of carnal thoughts. The carnal mind is an enemy to God and cannot please Him. When we are alive in Christ, we are dead to sin.

Paul writes more about suffering as a child of God in Romans eight. He said there is no guilt for those who are in Christ because we no longer walk in sin. He said the suffering of this life cannot be compared to the glory that will be revealed to us in eternity. Humans are subject to frailty and weakness, but we can be set free and receive new spiritual strength through Christ. We await the resurrection of our bodies from the grave when we shall be in the presence of Jesus. We hope for our upcoming resurrection with patience and composure.

The Holy Spirit helps us even when we don't know how to pray. The Spirit makes intercession for us with groaning that cannot be verbalized. Paul reassures us that all things work together for the good of those who know God. We may not understand our suffering and loss, but hold tight to your faith, as God knows what is best.

Paul asks in Romans 8:31, "If God be for us, who can be against us?" Foes may try to throw us off track, but God is with us. He is much stronger than Satan and all his angels. In the Last Day, God will destroy Satan and cast him into outer darkness in a bottomless pit. Nothing can ever separate us from God's everlasting love.

Paul writes about God's mercy in Romans 9:16-19. God's gift of mercy cannot be compared to human will or effort. His compassion for His children is unequalled. He has mercy on the one who is turning from sin to salvation. He can harden our spirits so we can serve Him without falling away. He can mold our lives like a lump of clay in the potter's hands. He can take a sinful life and transform it into a thing of beauty. His mercy is always available when we come to Him.

Israel turned their backs on God and backslid in Romans nine and ten. Each time Israel failed God, He would save a remnant of believing Jews who could eventually come back and rebuild destroyed walls and temples. In Romans 11:4, God said He had reserved seven thousand men who had not bowed to the idol god Baal. God can take a remnant, the elect and chosen; and He can restore lives and nations into a beautiful tapestry that brings honor and glory to His name.

Sacrifice is a part of our service to God. He showed us His sacrificial offering at the cross, so we are to offer Him our sacrificial love in return. Paul challenged the Roman Christians in Romans 12:1, "I beseech you therefore, brethren, by the mercies of God, that ye present your bodies a living sacrifice, holy, acceptable unto to God, which is your reasonable service." He begged them to make a conscious decision to give their all to God. Paul said this is the rational and reasonable thing to do in light of God's mercy toward us.

He tells us to not be conformed to this world but be transformed through a renewed mind. This transformation is proof that we seek God's perfect will for our life. This decision comes from our mind and heart as we dedicate ourselves to His service. Paul challenges us to use the gifts and talents God has given to further His kingdom on earth. Our talents differ, but we are to work together in unity as one spiritual body for the good of Christ.

We are to always exhibit behavior fitting of a child of God. Love should be sincere, pure, and without hypocrisy; kindly affectionate showing honor to one another; we are to be aglow with the Spirit as we serve God; rejoice in the hope that comes from knowing Christ; be steadfast and patient in suffering; constant in prayer; giving freely to the needs of other believers; practice hospitality; bless those who persecute us; rejoice with those who rejoice and weep with those who weep; living in harmony with others; serve humbly; and live at peace with everyone. Paul said we should never come up short in our zeal for the Lord; we must bless and not curse others; don't be snobbish or exclusive; don't repay evil with evil; and don't be overcome by evil. It is impossible if we try to meet these standards on our own power; we must depend on God to allow the Holy Spirit to guide our steps and behavior in every area of life.

Paul tells us in Romans 13:12 to cast off the works of darkness and put on the armor of light. We are to put on the Lord Jesus, and not give in to lustful desires. Paul said in Romans 14:7 that none of us lives or dies to himself. We live and die to the Lord because we belong to Him. Jesus is the Lord of the living and the dead. There is coming a day when every knee shall bow to the Lord and every tongue shall confess to God (Romans 14:11). We will each give an account to God.

Paul loved the people in Rome although he had not visited them yet. There is a natural but God-given love for fellow-believers even though we may not know them personally. We are bound together in the bond of Christ's love because we are a part of the same spiritual body and heritage.

Chapter Eight

The Book of Galatians

Paul had a three-fold reason for writing to the church he planted in Galatia.

1. To underscore the doctrine of justification by faith,
2. To prove his divine appointment as an apostle,
3. To warn Christians against a return to Judaism.

The book of Galatians has been called the Magna Carta of the church. In 1215, King John in England granted a Magna Carta that guaranteed certain rights and liberties to businessmen and church leaders by limiting the power of the king.

In Paul's letter, he intended to argue for Christian liberty in the face of false teachers in the church. The unbelieving Jews argued that people needed to obey the Old Testament Law as a part of the plan of salvation. Paul was more than capable to defend Christians when they accepted God's plan of salvation that is free from the Law.

Paul made it clear in Galatians 1:10-16 that he had been called through a revelation by Christ to preach the Gospel. When Saul received Christ in Damascus, he knew he was being called from being a persecutor to preach the saving power of Jesus Christ. He did not receive a message from a man to preach, but by a divine revelation. Saul, the persecutor, created havoc in the church by having Christians bound in chains and taken to Jerusalem for a hearing and punishment because of their faith in Christ.

Christ chose and set Saul apart before he was born to proclaim the message of salvation to the Gentiles. Jesus' apostles or any other man had any part in Paul's calling by Christ to preach. Paul's testimony would hopefully convince the Christians in Galatia of his divine appointment. Jesus' other apostles accepted Paul as an apostle in First Corinthians 2:9.

In Galatians, Paul speaks frequently about the cross and the resulting faith, grace, and mercy that flow freely from God to anyone who wants to accept His gift. Paul told the church in Galatians 5:1, "Stand fast therefore in the liberty wherewith Christ hath made us free and be not entangled again with the yoke of bondage." Christ liberated us and set us free from sin and the Law. We have new-found liberty and freedom in Christ Jesus. The believing Jews were slaves to the Law, but now had a new freedom in Christ. Believing Gentiles also enjoyed their freedom in Christ.

The Jews argued that Gentile males must be circumcised to be a believer in Jesus, but Paul refuted this argument. He said there was no advantage for circumcision because of our freedom in Christ. The Jews who were circumcised were obligated to follow the whole Law, but this is unnecessary for Christians because Christ came to fulfil the Law. We don't rely on the Law but are guided in faith by the Holy Spirit. We have an active faith that is energized and expressed through a genuine love for Christ.

Paul made a very powerful statement in First Corinthians 5:13 when he said, "For, brethren, ye have been called unto liberty; only use not liberty for an occasion to the flesh, but by love serve one another." Our liberty in Christ comes with accountability to God and one another. Our freedom in Christ does not permit us to sin, for we have been saved from our sins. Freedom in Christ is not to be construed as freedom to sin. Paul made it clear that we must walk in the spirit so we do not fulfill the lust of the flesh (Galatians 5:16).

Paul defended the doctrine of justification (*reckoned righteousness*) by faith apart from the Law in Galatians three through five. He asked them if they received the Holy Spirit from the Law or by hearing the message of the Gospel. He reminded them they did not reach spiritual maturity by depending on the Law after starting their Christian walk with the Holy Spirit.

He wrote in Galatians 2:16, "Knowing that a man is not justified by the works of the law, but by the faith of Jesus Christ, even we have believed in Jesus Christ, that we might be justified by the faith of Christ, and not by the works of the law; for by the works of the law shall no flesh be justified." Paul then testified in Galatians 2:20 as he said, "I am crucified with Christ: nevertheless I live; yet not I, but Christ liveth in me: and the life which I now live in the flesh, I live by the faith of the Son of God, who loved me, and gave himself for me." It is faith, not the works of the Law that we come to Jesus for salvation. We die a spiritual death just as Christ died physically to become one of His.

All Jews correctly held Abraham, the father of the Jewish nation, in high regard. Paul told them Abraham relied on his strong faith in God, not the Law. They lived under the curse of the Law, but Christians are forgiven of sin and live under God's love, mercy, and grace. Galatians 3:13 tells us that Christ has redeemed us (*set us free*) from the curse of the law when He became a curse for us on the cross. Therefore, we are blessed by God as we share in Abraham's faith.

Those living under the Law face disappointment and destruction as they cannot keep the full Law. The Law was intended to point out guilt due to their transgressions, but believers enjoy freedom from the guilt of sin because Christ's blood has cleansed us from all sin (1 John 1:7). We have become sons of God when we accept His Son as our Savior.

Paul assures us in Galatians 4:7 that we are no longer a servant to the Law, but a son and an heir of God through

Christ Jesus. Christians are adopted sons of God. We now know God and are known by Him. Paul told the Gentile Christians he was a Jew but had become like them when he accepted Christ.

Paul warned in Galatians 4:17-18 that the Jewish teachers were trying to dazzle them to turn from Christ back to Judaism. The false teachers wanted to isolate the Christians for no good purpose. He encouraged them to let Christ mold them into the person they ought to be. To turn from Christ back to Judaism would mean the loss of their freedom in Christ, and would make His sacrifice on the cross meaningless. Paul's prayer for them was that the grace of Jesus would meld into their spirit so they could become one with Christ.

Paul urged the Gentile Christians in Galatians 5:1 to stand fast in the liberty they received when Christ set them free from the bondage of sin. We are not to become entangled again with the yoke of bondage once Christ sets us free. Our liberty in Christ should motivate us to also serve others. We are to walk in the Holy Spirit rather than pursue the lust and sin Satan uses to tempt us.

Paul lists the fruits of the Spirit in Galatians 5:22-23: love, joy, peace, longsuffering, gentleness, goodness, faith, meekness, and temperance. The law of Christ guides us into these positive steps as we serve and interact with others.

We are to bear one another's burdens. If our brother fails in his walk, we are to try and restore him rather than judge or criticize. We are warned in Galatians 6:7 to not be deceived, as whatsoever we sow, we shall also reap. We are not to grow weary as we strive to serve God and others, for we will reap our reward in due time.

Paul closes his letter by saying, "But God forbid that I should glory, save in the cross of our Lord Jesus Christ, by whom the world is crucified unto me, and I unto the world (Galatians 6:14)." Paul's focus was on Christ, not his personal suffering for Jesus' sake. He prayed for God's peace and grace to be with them. We too are to serve unselfishly as we carry out Christ's mission.

Chapter Nine

The Book of Ephesians

The central theme of Paul's letter to the church at Ephesus was to be united in Christ. A divided church is ineffective when it comes to growth and outreach to others. When outsiders see division and disagreement, they shy away from the church.

Christ chose us before creation that we should serve Him in love without blame. Christ predestined us to be His children. In Him we have redemption and forgiveness through His blood according to the richness of His grace *(underserved favor)*. He has made known to us the mystery of His will (Ephesians 1:3-9). He predestined whosoever will accept His gift of forgiveness and His living hope of eternal life.

In Ephesians 1:10, Paul said, "That in the dispensation of the fullness of times he might gather together in one all things in Christ, both which are in heaven, and which are on earth; even in him." Christ will bring His plan to full completion in the end time. He will gather all His saints together for eternity. He will deal Satan a final blow which was God's plan from the outset. The Holy Spirit is our guarantee of our inheritance that Christ purchased with His blood.

Paul paints a sad picture of people who serve Satan in Ephesians two. We followed Satan, the prince of this world, who controlled our thoughts and actions. We were rebellious and disbelieved in Christ. We pursued our passions and cravings to satisfy our fleshly desires, giving us no hope without God.

The good news is that God through His intense love made us alive when we accepted Christ. We took on the image of Christ when we were buried with Him in baptism. We become partners with Christ in His death and resurrection when we are baptized. We are buried in the water and come forth as if we are resurrected. When Jesus comes back, we will receive a new glorified body that will never die, just like His. We have become an heir of God and a joint-heir with Christ to all God's riches which cannot be measured or quantified.

Ephesians 2:8 says, "For by grace are ye saved through faith; and that not of yourselves: it is the gift of God." We don't deserve salvation, but by faith we can receive it as a gift from God. We are delivered from judgment and become partakers of Christ's salvation through faith. We cannot earn salvation through good works or effort, as it is a gift of God. We can only boast in Christ that He paid our sin debt on Calvary's cross.

We can walk by His side instead of being a great distance from Christ. He is our bond of unity as He brings Jews and Gentiles together under His umbrella of love. The hostile wall that separates people has been broken down so all people globally can serve Him as one body.

Paul said in Ephesians 2:16, "And that he might reconcile both unto God in one body by the cross, having slain the enmity thereby." The cross unites us into one church to serve Him. The cross and the empty tomb are like a magnet that draws us together in Christ. When Jesus comes back, He will merge all nationalities together as we praise Him in unison in a heavenly chorus.

The church has members from all levels of society and economic circumstances. The members are diverse in many ways, but in Christ and His cross we become one body in Him. The church is to be a unified body that functions much like the human body. The various members of the human body function differently but work in concert. When we eat, the teeth chew the food and the digestive tract breaks it down so the nutrients can be harvested for the good of the body. The foot cannot perform the function of the hand, and vice-versa. The church also functions in much the same manner. Each member is accountable to do their best for the Lord so the entire body is blessed and strengthened. The united body of Christ becomes a permanent dwelling place for God.

It was natural for Jews who converted from Judaism to

Christianity to have different views from Gentile believers. We cannot escape the fact we are largely products of our heritage. The Jews were observers of the Old Testament Law prior to accepting Christ, while the Gentiles were considered as pagan heathens. Christ came to bring them together as one.

Christ is a mystery to many. We may not fully understand that He is our Creator, our Savior, and Redeemer, but He is. Faith enables us to accept mysteries we don't understand. It is impossible for a human to be as great as Christ. He was appointed and anointed by God to be our all-in-all, our King of kings, and Lord of lords. Paul reveals the mystery of Christ in Ephesians three. The mystery to the Jews was that Jesus came to earth to seek and to save the lost regardless of nationality or social standing. They were jealous when the Gospel was preached to the Gentiles, for they had been declared as God's chosen people. The mystery to them was that the Gentiles were now their fellow-heirs of the same body, and partakers of His promise in Christ through the Gospel (Ephesians 3:6-7). The unbelieving Jews had no desire to understand or accept what Paul told them.

There was a purpose in the mystery. Paul considered himself unworthy to preach the unsearchable riches of Christ to the Gentiles. The mystery had existed from the very beginning of the ages by God who created all things through Christ. A part of the mystery was that the wisdom of God would be made known by the church to all people. God's purpose and plan became a reality through Jesus Christ in whom Paul had a holy boldness and confidence because of his faith (Ephesians 3:8-12).

Paul's prayer was that God would grant the church inner strength through the Holy Spirit so they would be rooted and grounded in God's love. He wanted them to know the love of Christ that surpasses all knowledge, so they could be fully blessed. He said God can do exceedingly abundantly above all we ask or think, through the power He gives us (Ephesians 3:14-20).

Paul was a prisoner of Christ. Every believer has been freed as a slave to Satan to become a prisoner of Christ who gives us all liberty and spiritual freedom. He said there is one body, one Spirit, one Lord, one faith, and one baptism where we are called in one hope of our calling. We gratefully accept what God gives us without seeking substitutes or fully understanding His mysteries. Christ is our bridge from sin to salvation.

In Him we see where unity in the church is required if the church is to reflect His light of love and forgiveness to those lost in sin. Every Christian is accountable to God to live a pure and blameless life so others will see our individual light. When all Christians come together as one, the light into our communities is magnified since we are all working together to fulfill Christ's mission to seek and save the lost.

Ephesians 4:13 is a key verse in Paul's letter. He wrote, "Till we all come in the unity of the faith, and of the knowledge of the Son of God, unto a perfect man, unto the measure of the stature of the fullness of Christ." When we learn who Jesus is as God's Son and embrace Him as our Savior, we can then become mature Christians who are equipped to do His work. We grow as Christians as we learn more about

Him and follow His example of love for us. We are united in our faith and knowledge of Christ. A united church is a strong voice for right in a world of wrong.

Paul warns the Ephesians in Chapter five verses 25-31 to not grieve the Holy Spirit. One of the first requirements of not grieving the Spirit is to deal only in the truth. A falsehood offends our fellow man and grieves the Spirit. If we get upset, we are to dismiss anger and wrath before sundown the same day. The devil must not be given an open door to creep into our lives. Dishonest thieves are to get a job to earn a living rather than stealing. The Holy Spirit cannot condone a filthy or slandering tongue. We are to dismiss bitterness, a bad temper, resentment, quarreling, and abuse. All these bad things must be replaced with kindness, helpfulness, compassion, and forgiveness.

In Ephesians five, Paul lists three specific aspects of our Christian walk. Paul refers to Christians as dear children that he is teaching how to walk with Christ.

- And walk in love, as Christ also hath loved us, and hath given himself for us an offering and a sacrifice to God for a sweet-smelling savor (Ephesians 5:2).
- For ye were sometimes darkness but are now ye light in the Lord: walk as children of light (Ephesians 5:8).
- See then that ye walk circumspectly (*prudently*), not as fools, but as wise (Ephesians 5:15).

Our walk with and for Christ is to be one filled with love, light, prudence, and wisdom. When we are laser-focused on doing His will, we can receive His blessings that cannot be found elsewhere.

In the latter part of Ephesians chapter five and the first nine verses of chapter six, Paul lists the duties of husbands, wives, and children. It was Paul's desire that families be united and working together. A united family is very similar to a united church. Each member is to perform their individual duties for the benefit of the entire family. If either parent neglects their duty, the whole family suffers discord and disunity. The children suffer when a parent lets down on their responsibility. Each family member is to be respected and honored as individuals. God blesses families who are united and serving Christ together.

The strength of a nation is defined largely by the strength of its families. Strong family units add to the strength of the nation. Divorce, death, and neglect unfortunately can take their toll on family units.

Paul concludes his letter to the church at Ephesus with words of encouragement. He said in Ephesians 6:10-18 that we need to realize we are in warfare with Satan and his angels. He encourages us to be strong in the Lord, and to rely on His power and might. We are to dress for battle against the rulers of darkness and spiritual wickedness in high places. Our spiritual body armor includes truth, righteousness, the gospel of peace, a strong faith in God, salvation, and the Word of God. These are our weapons of war to be used against Satan.

Many people may not understand the spiritual battle that is being waged for their souls. Others may not be equipped to wage spiritual warfare with Satan because of a weak faith. Paul says we can take steps to stand strong in the Lord, but we must train and prepare for the battle.

Paul told the Christians at Ephesus he was praying constantly for them. It is comforting to know someone is praying for us. Paul knew the power of prayer and he depended on God to have a watchful eye on the Christians in Ephesus.

His desire was to have boldness to continue preaching the mystery of the Gospel as an ambassador in bonds. Paul's imprisonment did not deter him in telling the Roman guards and his fellow inmates about the saving power of Jesus Christ.

Paul's closing benediction for the saints in Ephesus is found in Ephesians 6:23-24: "Peace be to the brethren, and love with faith, from God the Father and the Lord Jesus Christ. Grace be with all them that love our Lord Jesus Christ in sincerity. Amen."

Chapter Ten

Paul's Letter to the Philippians

On his second mission trip, Paul met Lydia on a riverbank as she worshiped and prayed with a group of other women (Acts 16:12). Paul baptized Lydia and her family that same day.

A little later, Paul and Silas were arrested, beaten, and their feet were locked in stocks in a prison dungeon. (See details of the jailer's conversion in Chapter Three, Philippi, Macedonia).

Paul planted a New Testament church in Philippi with the help of Lydia and the jailer. He had a deep love and affection for the church. His letter to them sometime later was to encourage them in their walk of unity, holiness, and the resulting joy they found in Christ. He had fond memories of past days working and preaching in Philippi, and he prayed for them often. He referred to the fellowship in the Gospel that he enjoyed while working with them. Paul was confident that God who began a good work in the church at Philippi would continue well into the future.

Paul was a prisoner when he wrote the book of Philippians. He had defended the Gospel and had been arrested because of the message of a risen Savior. Paul was homesick to see the Philippians once again. He prayed for them that their love would thrive and grow as they gained more knowledge about Christ and His love for fallen man. He wanted them to continue to strive for excellence in their walk with the Lord until their earthly life ended. He prayed they would also strive to be righteous as they served the Lord.

Paul let them know that although he was a prisoner, the Gospel continued being taught by him to the people in the palace and other places. His imprisonment did not mean he would stop teaching and preaching about Christ to whatever audience he had. He did not let jail time become down time. He was faithful to God regardless of his circumstances. His imprisonment meant he would witness to fellow inmates who otherwise may never hear about the saving grace of Jesus. Paul's captivity encouraged other teachers and preachers to speak out more boldly for Christ. Paul rejoiced that the Word was being preached.

Paul was not ashamed of Christ or the Gospel. He said in Philippians 1:20, "According to my earnest expectation and my hope that in nothing I shall be ashamed, but that with all boldness, as always, so now also Christ shall be magnified in my body, whether it be by life, or by death." Paul's commitment to Christ was for his entire earthly life span regardless of the outcome. He had committed himself to the preaching of the Gospel until his dying day. He said in Philippians 1:21, "For to me to live is Christ, and to die is gain." Paul was confident that his soul would go to Paradise when he breathed his final breath. He did not fear death because his hope and confidence was in the Lord.

Paul understood his earthly ministry was incomplete. He found himself caught between a desire of staying on earth or going to Paradise. He wanted to depart this life to be with Christ, but he was willing to remain on earth as long as the Lord needed him here.

Paul found abundant joy in serving Christ in all circumstances.

He encouraged the Christians in the Philippian church to stand fast in the Holy Spirt and serve God with one mind. They needed unity as a church as they continued to spread the Gospel. He told them to not be afraid of the enemies of the church but continue preaching the salvation of God. Paul told them to be prepared to suffer for Christ's sake, just as he was suffering when he wrote to them.

In Philippians two, Paul wrote about humility, unity, and witnessing. He had learned the lesson of humility when he was beaten, imprisoned, ship wrecked, and had to run for his life. His desire for the Christians in Philippi is summed up in Philippians 2:2-4 when he wrote, "Fulfil ye my joy that ye be like-minded, having the same love, being of one accord, of one mind. Let nothing be done through strife or vainglory (*pride*); but in lowliness of mind let each esteem (*the*) other better than themselves. Look not every man on his own things, but every man also on the things of others." He is saying, "Let's all love God and man with a genuine love and get along with each other." When Christians focus on loving God, there is no room for other distractions such as pride, arrogance, or selfishness.

Paul told them in Philippians 2:5-11 to look at the example set by Christ on humility. Christ did not come from heaven to earth to be applauded by man, but he took upon Himself the role of a servant and came in the likeness of a man. He was the divine Son of God who came to us as our Son of man. He was equal with God before He came to earth, but He stepped out of that divine role to

become human. This took a great
deal of humility that deserves our full
attention. Jesus died as a man on
the cross, but He came forth from
death in a new glorified body. He
became equal to God again when He
was resurrected.

While on earth, He became obedient
even unto death on the cross.
Because of His unselfishness on the
cross, God exalted Him with a name
that is above all other names. This
gives Jesus power, dominion, and
greatness above all others. He
deserves sincere worship from every
person on earth for who He is and
what He did for us as our sacrificial
Lamb. His resurrection from death
gives every believer the hope of a
personal resurrection when Jesus
comes to claim His bride, the church.

Philippians 2:10-11 says that on the
day Jesus comes back, "That at the

name of Jesus every knee should bow, of things in heaven, and things in earth, and things under the earth; and that every tongue should confess that Jesus Christ is Lord, to the glory of God the Father." There will be universal agreement that Jesus is Lord when every tongue confesses. Even unbelievers will confess Him as Lord.

On his second mission trip when Paul planted a new church in Philippi, he laid out God's plan of salvation. He now tells them in his letter, that based on God's plan, to work out their own salvation with fear and trembling. They were to cultivate and complete their personal salvation with an awesome fear according to God's plan. They were to distrust their own sufficiency and do all they could to bring credit to God for their salvation; for it is God who provided our salvation through

himself." God raised Jesus from death on the third day after His crucifixion on the cross. That day Jesus' body was transformed from a corruptible, decaying body to a glorified, incorruptible body that will never die. Our earthly mortal bodies that are constantly dying will be changed on resurrection day to heavenly, glorified bodies just like Christ's. Glorified bodies will never see death. Our citizenship will transfer from earth to a heavenly citizenship when we enter into the joys of our Lord.

Paul loved the church in Philippi according to Philippians 4:1. He called them his joy and crown, so he encouraged them to stand fast in the Lord. Our walk must be steadfast and sure with Christ. We walk through a world of darkness and sin, but His light shows us the way. Psalm 119:105 says, "Thy word is a lamp unto my feet, and a light unto my path." God's Word, the Bible, is to also be our lamp and light. When we read His Word, the Holy Spirit can speak and guide us in God's truth.

There were several women who had helped Paul in his ministry. He asked the church to pray for these faithful fellow-servants whose names are written in the book of life in heaven. He told the Christians to always rejoice in the Lord. We are to be happy and glad for what Christ did for us on the cross. We need to rejoice at the promise of eternal life with Him. We should never take things for granted as we pray with thankfulness and make our requests known to God. His peace will dwell in our hearts as we seek a close walk with God and His Son Jesus.

Paul points our attention in Philippians 4:8-9 to truth, honesty, justice, purity, lovely things, and a good reputation. As Christians, we need to think on and practice these virtues. We are to praise God for giving us these road-marks that are like a map so we can live excellent lives for Him. They are God's standards for His children.

Paul saw both success and failure in his ministry for Christ. He experienced want and plenty; safety and danger; exaltation and humility; fullness and hunger. He knew what it was to be in want and to have plenty. Through all his trials, Paul never lost faith. He learned to be content with whatever circumstances he faced. He made a powerful statement that we need to embrace in Philippians 4:13, "I can do all things through Christ which strengtheneth me." His trust and confidence was in the Lord to protect and sustain him through every trial and situation. Paul had to rely on Christ to give him the daily strength needed for his ministry.

The church at Philippi had been faithful financial supporters of Paul during his mission trips. They had sacrificed so Paul's ministry could extend to other parts of Asia Minor. Paul told them in Philippians 4:19, "But my God shall supply all your need according to his riches in glory by Christ Jesus." It is comforting to know our needs will be met according to and not out of God's fullness. We are joint-heirs with Christ to all God's riches. He supplies our daily needs and we need to give Him praise and show our gratitude for His provision every day.

Chapter Eleven

The Book of Colossians

Paul's letter to the church at Colosse in Asia Minor was written to reiterate the preeminence (*superiority*) of Christ. Jesus is superior to every other person on earth, and He is the Head of His church. His superiority exceeds the greatest presidents, popes, kings, and preachers. No one in the present or the past can equal Christ, as He is equal to God (John 5:18). Paul wanted to encourage the church to keep their focus on Christ as Lord, and not let false teaching and worldly speculation dim their view of Him.

Apparently Paul had not visited Colosse on any of his mission trips as he said in Colossians 1:4, "Since we heard of your faith in Christ Jesus, and of the love which ye have to all the saints." Then he said in Colossians 2:1, many in Colosse had not seen his face. Epaphras was the faithful minister at the church in Colosse (Colossians 1:7). Although Paul had not been to their city, he still prayed regularly for them. He could relate to them as he had heard about their faith and love for Christ. All Christians globally share the same universal hope that is laid up for us in heaven because of our common belief in the Bible. Paul's intent in writing his letter was to encourage them in the faith and help them grow stronger in the Lord.

Paul sets forth his case for Christ as the Head of the Church in Colossians 1:12-18:

- He brings us together to be partakers of the saint's inheritance,

- He has delivered us from the power of darkness and sin, and translated us into His kingdom,
- He has redeemed us through His blood, and forgiven our sins,
- He is the image of the invisible God, and is the firstborn of every creature,
- By Him He created everything in heaven and on earth, visible and invisible, including thrones, dominions, principalities (*a prince's area of rule*), and powers. All things were created by and for Him.
- He pre-existed all things before creation, and in Him all things exist.
- He is the head of the body, the church,
- He is the firstborn of the dead when He came forth from death

after His crucifixion; therefore, He is preeminent and superior.

How could anyone argue against His majesty, divinity, and superiority?

It gave God great pleasure that in Christ everything is complete. There is nothing lacking that we need from Him, for He has the power to help us with every problem and meet every need. His shed blood on the cross reconciles wayward sinners to God and gives us a peace that cannot be described in human terms. We can be separated and alienated from God because of evil works, but Christ's blood reconciles us to Him. He has the power to make us holy, unblameable, and unreproveable in His sight if we are fully committed. Because of His gracious gift, we are to be grounded and settled in Christ. Paul preached a message of hope that all Christians worldwide cherish.

Paul then wrote about sacrificial service to Christ. He knew all about extreme suffering for the sake of Christ. He reminded them of the suffering Christ endured for every believer's benefit. Paul reminded them of his call from God as a minister to preach the Word that had been a mystery for many through the centuries. The mystery of the Gospel includes at least seven major subjects:

- The mystery of creation,
- The mystery of the prosperity of the wicked,
- The mystery of God's providential care,
- The mystery of a spiritual rebirth in Christ,
- The mystery of being one in Christ,

- The mystery of suffering for Christ's sake,
- The mystery of eternity with Christ.

Because Jesus came to earth, suffered greatly, was murdered, arose from the dead, and ascended back to the Father in heaven, the hidden mysteries are now unveiled. When we study the Bible, we learn about God's love for fallen man. Without His love and His gift of Christ the mysteries would go unsolved.

Paul had an inward struggle (*conflict*) for the saints in Colosse, Laodicea, and other churches that had not met him. Paul's sincere concern that these who had never met him would be bound together in cords of love and be blessed fully through the conviction of their faith; so they could understand completely God's mysteries including Christ, the anointed of God. The treasures of divine wisdom and insight into His ways and purposes were stored up and hidden for many. Even those who believe in Christ may not fully understand all the mysteries of God. Paul's concern was that some silver-tongued orator may try and persuade the new Jewish converts to not follow Christ and revert to Judaism.

Paul was encouraged when he heard of their steadfast faithful service and commitment to Christ. Their faith allowed them to have an absolute trust and confidence in Christ's power, wisdom, and goodness. Paul encouraged them to walk in lock-step with Christ each day. He wanted them to be like mighty trees with deep roots in Christ. He wanted their faith in Christ to thrive and flourish and overflow with thanksgiving.

There was a real danger that some philosopher or other worldly person could come into their church and teach worldly traditions that were not in keeping with Christ's truth and standards. It is in Christ alone that we dwell in the fullness of God. We are complete in Him because He is the head over all men.

Paul then addresses again the subject of circumcision in Colossians 2:11. He said believers are circumcised without hands through Christ. We have put off and expelled the old sinful person we used to be before we accepted Christ. Paul says this came about through our baptism into Christ. The Jews were dead in trespasses and circumcision of the flesh, but Christ has made His believers alive by forgiving all sin. God erased man's requirements of the Law for salvation and nailed them to the cross of Christ.

Christ reigns victorious over all earthly powers and Satan. No one except God has powers equal to Christ. Paul told them to not let anyone judge them over their daily behavior. Christ is the substance of all we think or do, so our lives cannot be questioned. They were not to let anyone umpire their lives and rob them of their treasure in Christ. No person can disqualify us from the prize that awaits us in heaven.

We are to stay implanted in Christ and hold fast to Him. We are to be knit together in Christ as one and grow in His knowledge and grace. Paul asked in Colossians 2:20 if we have died with Christ and given up material ways of looking at things, and have escaped from the world's crude notions, why we still live as if we belong to the world. It is futile to cling to the things of the world while trying to serve Christ. These worldly excesses are popular with unbelievers but are of no benefit to a believer of Christ. We have graduated from the lower nature of sinful man to a higher plane with Christ. We no longer need to indulge in worldly excesses to find peace and contentment.

Believers are to shift gears from the earthly to the heavenly. We are to think on things above, much more than the things on earth. Our new life in Christ is secure in Him. When Christ comes back to earth we will be with Him for eternity. Our glorified bodies will have a glowing radiance and splendor like His. Paul tells us to kill the evil desires that tempt us to stray from Christ. Believers are strong in spirit and desire, but we have the tendency of being weak in the flesh. Paul warns us to not let passion exceed our commitment to Christ. Sin causes God to be jealous and have a holy anger if we obstinately oppose His divine will for our life.

At one time, we walked in sin before accepting Christ, but we are told to rid ourselves of anger, rage, improper feelings toward others, cursing, slander, foulmouthed abuse, lying, and shameful words. We are to constantly strive to let the Holy Spirit mold us and make us into fit vessels for Christ. We are made in the image of God, so it pleases Him when we strive to be more like Him.

There are to be no distinctions on skin color, nationalities, and social or economic standing. Christ is above all and in all without preferences toward anyone. We are all equal in God's sight. Every person can come to Christ in repentance and receive Him as Lord. Christ looks on us all in pity and mercy. He is patient and longsuffering with His children.

We are told to have a forgiving spirit with one another, for the Lord has forgiven us. His patience is enduring with those who strive to follow Him. Love binds us together in complete and ideal harmony. Our souls become harmonious with Christ as we strive to pattern our lives after His. We can praise God that we have been made one in Christ. His word is to be the nutrient to feed our souls daily. Our worship to God is to be filled with thanksgiving and praise. We have no reason to feel neglected or downtrodden because we are now one of His.

Every thought and action should be pleasing to Christ because we are depending on Him and the Holy Spirit to guide us in all things. Wives, husbands, and children must work together in love and respect for one another, for this pleases the Lord. Fathers are not to harass or provoke their children to withdrawal or anger, lest they become discouraged. Discipline is not intended to make a child feel inferior or frustrated. We don't need to break a child's spirit to make a point on discipline (Colossians 3:21).

When we work for others, we are to give our efforts one hundred percent. We are to serve our superiors with obedience and respect unless they ask us to do something immoral. Our Master in heaven is Jesus Christ, and He will give us our final reward for a job well-done at the Last Day. The master and the slave are equal in God's sight, for every soul is precious to Him.

Earthly masters should realize they have a heavenly Master who will be their final Judge. We will be judged for the deeds done on earth. Romans 2:6 says, "Who will render to every man according to his deeds." This is referring to the final judgment.

We are to have a steadfast prayer life, be alert, thankful, and intent in our prayers. Paul was in prison when he wrote this letter, so he asked the Christians in Colosse to pray that God would open a door so he could proclaim the mystery concerning Christ. He knew it was his duty to tell others the good news of the Gospel, but he was being hampered while in prison in Rome. The door to ministry was temporarily shut for Paul, but he knew there is nothing that is impossible with God.

He encouraged the Christians in Colosse to behave with prudence and discretion with others. We have the opportunity to witness to others though our words and actions. We need to seize the opportunity to witness as God opens the doors. Our words need to be pure and clean so we don't mislead anyone away from Christ. If someone asks us why we are a believer, we are to tell them what Christ has done and is doing in our life. Our testimony and example may mean more to the hearer than anything else at that moment in time.

Paul closed his letter by sending four of his fellow-workers to give the church in Colosse a first-hand account of what had been going on in Rome. Several other co-workers of Paul including Justus, Luke, and Epaphras sent greetings to the church. He wanted the church to know how they had been faring and give them comfort and encouragement.

A short summary of the book of Colossians is:

- Serving Christ sacrificially;
- Serving Christ according to the Bible, not philosophy;
- Serving Christ instead of legalism;
- Serving Christ with a heavenly vs. earthly mind.

Paul's final charge to the church in Colosse was that they carefully discharge the duties of the ministry and fulfill the stewardship they had received from the Lord. He closed with a brief prayer that God's grace would be upon them.

Chapter Twelve

The Books of Thessalonians

Paul's First Letter to the Church in Thessalonica

It is believed First Thessalonians was possibly Paul's first letter to any of the new churches he planted. He could have written the epistle in First Thessalonians as early as A.D. 49 to A.D. 54 from Corinth. He wanted to encourage the Christians there to live clean lives. One of the major themes of the letter is to address the imminent return of Christ to earth. Paul hoped this would bring comfort and hope to everyone. His message still resonates with all believers globally, as we eagerly look forward to Christ's return to rapture His church.

Acts 17 gives a record of Paul's second mission trip when he visited Thessalonica and established a church. A few Jews and many Gentiles became believers and helped launch a strong church in spite of opposition to Paul and his message. Silvanus and Timothy were with Paul when he later wrote his letter to the church.

Paul said they prayed often for the church in Thessalonica. They remembered the church's work of faith, labor of love, and patience of hope in Christ. Paul was certain the church had been elected (*divinely appointed*) by God to do His work in Thessalonica.

Paul reiterated to the church his personal sincere commitment to the ministry. He preached the Word with conviction and power. Paul and his ministry team had proven themselves to be fit to preach the Word in simplicity and truth. The church responded to Paul's message with joy and full acceptance in the face of stiff persecution. The church members applied Paul's message that was inspired by the Holy Spirit, and they became examples for others in most of Greece to follow. The church's influence spread quickly throughout the entire region. The church was on fire for God. People gave the church credit for turning from idol worship to a full surrender to the real live God.

Paul had assurance the church was awaiting the return of Christ to earth. Christ had risen from the dead and ascended back to God in heaven forty days after His resurrection. The church embraced the power of God that worked through Christ that gives us an eternal hope. Paul also pointed out the awful fate of all unbelievers when Christ returns. We are privileged to be drawn to Christ and a new life in Him.

In First Thessalonians two, Paul reminded the church how fruitful his previous mission to their city had been. Some Jews and many Gentiles had accepted his message of forgiveness through Jesus Christ. They were motivated to establish a new church that was a shining light in their community. Paul was abused and persecuted when he preached the good news of the Gospel in Thessalonica, but he persevered and kept preaching. God gave Paul the strength to fight through conflict, pain, and stress. Paul's calling to preach was from God and he took His call seriously regardless of the outrageous actions by his opponents.

His intent was to please God, not man. God called Paul to preach, God gave him the message and the courage to preach, and God gave Paul the determination to always do the right thing. It is easy to let conflict be a distraction that can cause us to lose momentum in our walk with the Lord. We can use Paul's example to motivate us to a higher level of commitment to and service for God.

Paul was transparent in his ministry. He did not let flattery feed his ego. He did not have a thread of greed or selfishness. Paul was not in the ministry for profit, but his calling was to preach the Gospel to those who needed to know Christ as their Lord. Because of his high calling, Paul could have felt puffed up and privileged, but he remained humble so God could use him. Paul never put himself first or above his divine calling, as he stayed focused on God's call to preach. His behavior among the church members was reserved and proper as a minister. He was like a young mother giving nourishment to her baby. Paul treated the people with gentleness and kindness. Paul was more than their preacher; he shared his personal life with them so they would know his inner thoughts; for he had nothing to hide.

Paul struggled as he worked diligently in his tent-making business so he would not burden the church financially. He plied his business and his preaching with honor and commitment. The church witnessed Paul's blameless behavior as he relied on Christ to lead him each day. He led them like a father who urges his children to do their best at whatever they did. Paul pushed them to a higher level of excellence in their service to Christ. He wanted them to meet God's standards of excellence.

The reason the church at Thessalonica was so successful and focused on Christ is because they accepted Paul's Gospel message as if it were directly from God. They welcomed Paul's message and reacted to it in a very positive manner. The Word had a superhuman power and it motivated them into service for Christ. The church in Thessalonica became imitators of other successful churches in Judea. They had suffered the same kind of persecution as the Christians in Judea. Church growth came out of persecution. The message of Christ cannot be snuffed out by man because it is God-given.

Persecutors killed Jesus, the prophets, and harassed and drove Paul out. The church's enemies continue to openly make themselves an offense against God. They tried to hinder Paul from speaking to the Gentile nations so they could be saved. God would deal with their sinful ways in due time. Paul's desire was to re-visit Thessalonica to reconnect and fellowship with them. Paul was deterred from going back due to the work of Satan. Paul looked forward to the Last Day when all believers will stand in God's presence, and Satan will be destroyed. Christ will prevent Satan from ever bringing harm again.

Paul yearned to hear from the church in Thessalonica, but they did not communicate with him. Paul had been left behind and was alone in Athens, Greece when he wrote First Thessalonians three. He sent young

Timothy, who he considered as a brother, to go to Thessalonica to urge, comfort, and encourage them in their faith. Paul feared someone might mislead them because Paul had suffered for Christ so greatly. Paul felt God had allowed him to suffer, so he accepted his lot without any complaint. Paul had warned them when he was in Thessalonica earlier that his ministry team suffered affliction and difficulties. Paul was concerned that Satan would tempt and tell them Paul's ministry was bearing no fruit for the Lord.

He was encouraged when Timothy returned from Thessalonica and told him of the church's steadfast faith, their warm love, and their fond memories of him. This good news brought comfort and cheer because their faith in God had become evident to Paul. He gave thanks to God for the strength shown by the church in Thessalonica. He prayed for God to bless and grow their faith even more, and for His guidance on the church's spiritual journey. He wanted them to overflow in love for one another and for all people. Paul desired that their hearts would be faultless and pure in the sight of God. He reminded them that Jesus is coming back with His saints, the glorified people of God!

Paul had taught the people in Thessalonica how they should walk with the Lord. They knew when they walked with God they would be living a perfected life in Him. Paul taught them about the authority of Jesus Christ. He urged them to be consecrated *(separated and set apart)* for living a pure and holy life. They knew to abstain and shrink away from all sexual vices. This would enable them to control their own bodies as they separated from sinful things. They were not to pursue lustful passions like the heathen who were ignorant of God as if they had no knowledge of His will.

The Christians were urged to not defraud their brother, for the Lord will avenge all sin. God has not called us to impurity but to consecration. We are to dedicate ourselves to complete purity. To set this truth aside is to disregard God and His commands. God has given us the Holy Spirit and the Bible to guide us in all righteousness. Paul told them they had been taught God's command to love one another. They were encouraged to excel even more in their love for their fellow-man.

Paul urged them to live quiet and peaceful lives, to mind their own business, and work with their hands to earn a living. This would earn them the respect of their neighbors as they witnessed diligent efforts being made to provide for their families. They were to take care of their family's needs without depending on others.

Paul then addresses a very important message that offers us hope today about our loved ones who fall asleep in death. As believers, we have a hope in Christ that reaches beyond the grave. We believe Jesus died and rose again. God will allow Jesus to bring the believers who have fallen asleep in death with Him when He comes back! Jesus will descend from heaven with a loud cry of summons, with the shout of an archangel, and with the blast of the trumpet of God. The bodies of those who have departed this life in Christ will rise first from their resting places. The believers who are still alive when Jesus comes back will be caught up with the resurrected saints in the clouds to meet the Lord in the air. We will be with the Lord for all eternity. We are to comfort those who bereave the loss of a loved one with these words (1 Thessalonians 4:16-18).

He will come unexpectedly as a thief in the night. There will be no forewarning of His coming so men can make things right with God at the last moment. Saints will feel safe and secure when Jesus comes, but unbelievers will experience ruin and death. This is compared to a woman who is ready to give birth. Sometimes the labor pains come when least expected; Jesus will come with no pre-announcement.

Paul tells us we must not sleep as the unbelievers, but we must be alert and ready for His coming at any moment. Just think— He could come today! We need to be ready with a strong faith, love, and be full of hope.

Christ did not come to condemn us, but that we can obtain salvation through Him. He died for us so we can live eternally with Him. We are to use these words to encourage and uplift each other.

Paul tells the church to fully appreciate their faithful spiritual leaders even when they warn and urge them to a higher level of service. He tells church members to be faithful to warn and seriously advise those who are out of line, encourage the fainthearted, help those who are spiritually weak, and to be patient with everyone.

We are not to repay evil with evil but show kindness and seek goodness in all things. We are to be happy in our faith and always be joyful because of what Christ has done for us. We are to pray often and thank God for all blessings and trials. We are not to put a damper on the work of the Holy Spirit or hate the teachings found in the Bible, for they are truth. We are told again to abstain from all evil.

Paul's benediction for the church is found in First Thessalonians 5:23-28: "And the very God of peace sanctify you wholly; and I pray God your whole spirit and soul and body be preserved blameless unto the coming of our Lord Jesus Christ. Faithful is he that calleth you, who also will do it. Brethren, pray for us. Greet all brethren with an holy kiss. I charge you by the Lord that this epistle be read unto all the holy brethren. The grace of our Lord Jesus Christ be with you. Amen."

Paul's Second Letter to the Church at Thessalonica

Paul was probably still in Corinth when he wrote his second letter to the church in Thessalonica. Some of the things Paul said in his first letter about the coming of Christ had apparently been misunderstood by some. Paul wrote his second letter to clarify his claims about Christ coming back. He wanted to reconfirm the truth so they would not be confused.

Paul commended them because their faith in God and love for their neighbor was increasing. Paul told them he bragged on them to other churches because of their steadfastness, endurance, patience, and their strong faith in the face of distress and afflictions. They held up well to whatever circumstances they faced, and Paul encouraged them to keep doing the right things. He reassured them they would inherit God's kingdom due to their sincere walk. He said God will repay those who gave them problems. Rest and relief will come for all believers when Jesus comes again.

Paul said in Second Thessalonians 1:8-9 that Christ will come "in flaming fire taking vengeance on them that know not God, and that obey not the Gospel of our Lord Jesus Christ: who shall be punished with everlasting destruction from the presence of the Lord, and from the glory of his power." He will reward all believers with everlasting life and punish severely those who refuse to accept Him.

Paul's prayer was that God would count them worthy of this calling by fulfilling their work of faith with power: that the name of Christ is glorified in each believer according to His grace.

In Second Thessalonians two, Paul reiterated that the coming of the Lord had not yet come. He did not want them to be confused by what he wrote in his first letter about Jesus' return. He said Jesus will not come back until after a great falling away from the faith first occurs. Some believers will fall away from their faith in Christ and the church due to evil deceivers who will say Christ has already come. The great falling away in Greek is "apostasia" meaning apostasy. The man of sin (*antichrist)* will be revealed as one who exalted himself above God as he is the son of doom. He will take a seat in the temple and proclaim that he is God. He will be revealed for his lies in God's appointed time.

In the end time, there will be lawlessness against authority that is already at work in the world, but it will be restrained until the restrainer is taken out of the way. The antichrist will be revealed, and at Jesus' return He will slay him with the breath of His mouth and end his reign forever. Satan is behind the antichrist that will perform pretended miracles and signs which are all a bunch of lies. He will claim he is Christ. People will fall for his lies and refuse the truth that can save them from Satan.

God will send upon those who fall away from His truth and the church a strong delusion to make them believe what is false. There is a danger in hearing a falsehood enough that we finally accept a lie as truth. Judgment and condemnation will come upon all who follow the antichrist because they refused to believe Christ, the Truth. Pleasure in unrighteousness will take precedence over Truth before Jesus returns.

Paul told the believers they are loved by the Lord, and he gave thanks always for each one. God chose them from the beginning as some of the first converts to Christ. They found salvation through the sanctifying work of the Holy Spirit and their faith to trust Christ. The Gospel message Paul preached drew many to Christ. Consequently, all believers will share a glorified body with Christ when He returns. Paul encouraged them to stand firm and hold tightly the traditions and instructions they had been taught by Paul, by word, or by one of his two letters.

Above all else, Paul prayed for their comfort and courage as they continued serving Christ faithfully. He prayed for strength that they would remain steadfast and that God would keep them firmly on the right path with good words and works. In return, Paul asked that they pray for his ministry team that God's Word would spread rapidly and draw other new converts to Christ. The Thessalonians had gladly welcomed the Word, and Paul's strong desire was that others would be just as receptive.

Paul needed their prayers for deliverance from evil men because some reviled the truth. Paul said the Lord is faithful, and He gives strength and a sure foundation. He guards us from Satan and his angels. Paul was confident the Christians in Thessalonica would continue to do the things he had taught them. He prayed for the Lord to direct their hearts in showing God's love as they patiently awaited Christ's return to earth.

Paul charged them to stay away from believers who were shirkers instead of workers. They were to have no association with those who were lazy or disorderly. The church is like our body; all parts of the body must perform its function for the entire body to do well. The same is true of the church. Paul asked them to follow his example of how diligently they should work in the Lord's kingdom. Paul and his co-workers worked day and night so they would not have to burden the church for financial support. They would have been justified in receiving pay for their ministerial services, but they wanted to set a good example for the church to follow. Paul concluded that if a man refused to work, he should not eat.

Paul heard that some in the church were disorderly as they practiced idleness and neglected their Christian duty. They were busybodies rather than doing their own work. He encouraged the workers to not grow weary in doing right. He wanted them to be a strong example for others to follow. Paul felt disassociation with the lazy busy-bodies may cause them to be ashamed of their conduct. The lazy should be encouraged as a fellow believer.

Paul's benediction for the church is found in Second Thessalonians 3:16-18: "Now the Lord of peace himself give you peace always by all means. The Lord be with you all. The salutation of Paul with mine own hand, which is the token in every epistle: so I write. The grace of our Lord Jesus Christ be with you all. Amen."

Chapter Thirteen

Paul's Letters to Timothy

First Letter to Timothy

Timothy grew up in a God-fearing home with a mother who was very godly. Paul circumcised Timothy according to Jewish custom (Acts 16:3). Although Paul firmly believed circumcision was not a requirement for salvation, he felt they would be received by Jewish listeners more readily if Timothy was circumcised. This would break down a barrier as Paul and Timothy were both circumcised. Paul referred to Timothy as his son. Their main objective was to preach Christ so both Jews and Gentiles would believe their Gospel message.

Paul wrote Timothy to stay in Ephesus while he traveled to

Macedonia. Timothy was to warn and forbid certain individuals not to teach a different doctrine than the message he preached. These men were not to promote legends and endless genealogies. This would only promote speculation and questions rather than encouraging a strong faith and full reliance on God. Their absolute trust needed to be in God, not myths and fables.

Timothy was to encourage them to have pure love that flows from a sincere heart, a clear conscience, and an unfailing faith. Some had wandered away into vain arguments and discussions. Their message did not have purpose since it was not based on God's Word. These false teachers knew the Jewish Law and its rituals well, but they failed to understand what they were teaching. They would make unfounded assertions that meant nothing, and this could be very confusing to those who were trying to follow Christ, especially new converts.

Paul said the Law is good if it is followed as intended. The Law was not written for the upright and just, but for the lawless and unruly, the ungodly and sinful, the irreverent and profane, murderers of parents, impure and immoral, homosexuals, kidnappers, liars, and perjurers. The Law is designed to act as our judge when we disobey. Paul and Timothy's messages were on a much higher plane than the Law. They preached about the saving power of a forgiving Savior. Paul called it the glorious Gospel of the blessed God which had been entrusted to him to preach. The Law is our master, but God's grace sets us free from sin and legalism.

Paul was grateful to God who gave him strength and enabled him to travel and preach. Jesus had determined Paul could be trusted with the message and appointed him to the ministry. Paul was like a steward who was trying to enhance that with which he had been entrusted. His sole purpose was to spread the Gospel to as many as possible. Before his conversion, Saul did everything in his power to belittle and insult the church. Now he had made a complete turnaround which is called repentance. He received mercy from Jesus as he was ignorant when he persecuted Christians that he was completely outside the will of God. He was driven by ignorance and disbelief. He now realized it was grace that flowed freely that made the difference in his change for the good.

Paul called himself the chief of all sinners. Jesus came to earth to save sinners like him. Paul knew he could be an example for other renegade sinners to follow. He praised and gave God the glory as the only King eternal, immortal, invisible, and the only wise God. There was no question in Paul's mind about the power and magnificence of God, and he wanted to serve him to the fullest.

Paul charged Timothy to be a good warrior for Christ. He would have to fight battles to be able to preach the Word, just as Paul did. Paul encouraged young Timothy to have a strong faith and a good conscience. Some in the church had made a shipwreck of their lives because of a weak faith and immoral living.

He exhorted Timothy to pray intercessory prayers for kings and those in authority so they could lead a quiet and peaceful life because of godliness and honesty. God wants all men everywhere to be saved from sin and come to the knowledge of truth.

When we accept Christ, we can live in peace regardless of life's circumstances.

There is one God and Christ as our Mediator between God and man. Christ gave himself a ransom (*sin payment)* for all, to be testified in due time. Paul had been ordained as a preacher and apostle to tell others about the risen Lord and the forgiveness they could find in Him. He preached to Jews and Gentiles and many believed. This was the driving force in Paul's successful ministry.

He exhorted women to dress modestly and not overly adorn themselves with expensive jewelry and elaborate hair styles. He did not forbid all nice clothing or jewelry, but he wanted them to be a modest example as a godly woman to other women as they did good works. He said a woman should learn in silent study and should not teach or show authority over the man (1 Timothy 2:9-11). He referred to Adam being created first, and then Eve to underscore man's leadership role. He referred to their downfall when they committed the very first sin. Paul closed chapter two by briefly mentioning faith, love, and holiness with sobriety.

In First Timothy three, Paul tells Timothy the qualifications of a bishop *(elder)* in the church. An elder is an overseer of the spiritual affairs of the church. He should eagerly want to accept this responsibility to be an elder. This is not a position of honor, power, or authority, but is more about being a humble servant leader. An elder is to be the one to stand in the gap to keep out false teaching, contentions, and improper behavior. He must strive for excellence in his personal life and the care of the church.

Paul said an elder must have an impeccable reputation and be without blame; he must live above reproach and accusation; he is to only have one *(legal)* wife; be temperate and self-controlled; sensible and well behaved; dignified and lead an orderly disciplined life; hospitable, showing love to friends and strangers; capable and a qualified teacher; not given to wine; not combative but gentle and considerate; not quarrelsome but peaceable; not a lover of money gained through questionable means; and he should rule his household well keeping his children under control. Not many men can meet the Biblical requirements of an elder.

An elder should not be a new convert, as experience and knowledge of each member is needed. A man who is not ready for the leadership responsibilities may become discouraged and buckle under pressure when confronted with delicate problems that arise in the church. Their responsibilities include among other things the ministry staff, truthful teaching, church discipline, teaching the Scriptures, protecting the church against false teaching, uplifting and encouraging the discouraged, etc.

Paul then outlines the qualifications of a deacon in First Timothy 3:8-10. He must be worthy of respect; not a double-talker but sincere in what he says; not given to much wine, not greedy for gain through dishonest methods; have a strong faith with a clear conscience; proven worthy of the position; be above reproach; and the husband of one *(legal)* wife. Being a deacon is not a reward, but rather a man that supports the work of the elders. His responsibilities may include property maintenance, helping the destitute, assisting in worship services, etc. The first deacons were appointed specifically to help the church take care of the needs of widows.

Paul also wrote about the responsibilities of women in the church. They are to be worthy of respect, not gossip but temperate and self-controlled, and trust-worthy in all things. The elder's and deacon's wives play a very important support role so their husbands can perform their tasks without hindrance.

Paul gave the church these leadership instructions so each congregation could function well, even in his absence. Spreading the Gospel by the church was of paramount importance to Paul. He knew there had to be organization and structure in the church so she could carry out her mission.

He closed chapter three by re-focusing their attention on Christ. He talks about the mystery of godliness. This mystery was revealed as God was manifest in the flesh when He sent His Son to earth. Christ was justified and vindicated in the Holy Spirit, seen of angels, preached to the Gentiles, believed on in the world, and ascended back into heaven.

In First Timothy four, Paul comes back to the subject of apostasy *(great falling away)* in the church. This was a major concern to Paul since it is one of the things that will occur before the end of time on earth. The Holy Spirit had revealed and declared the upcoming apostasy to Paul. Demons will teach falsehoods that will draw people away from God.

People's minds will be as if they have been seared with a hot iron as they won't know the difference between the truth and a lie. The demons will forbid people to marry and teach them to avoid certain foods that God created for man's use. They will be unable to depend on truth but will follow the lies of demons. We are to receive God's blessings of food and many other blessings with thankful hearts. God's blessings are hallowed and holy and need to be accepted with thanksgiving.

It is the minister's responsibility to feed his flock with the truth of the faith. Preaching from the Bible should never be out of style or too old fashioned; for God's Word will never fade away like a fad. Ministers are to refuse and avoid irrelevant legends and silly myths. They need to take a firm stand and point out the fallacy of such teaching. A minister must stay spiritually strong through Bible study and prayer to be able to lead others in God's truth. A minister's spiritual strength is more important than his physical strength. He is like a ship's captain who helps us navigate through the storms of life. There is no room for Satan in the wheelhouse.

A preacher can be tempted to dilute the Gospel and preach a more acceptable and soothing message, but this is not according to God's will. Many people hunger to hear the truth, and ministers who don't preach the full Gospel miss a golden opportunity to tell people what they need and want to hear about God. We must hear the truth before we are convicted of sin so we can repent to God. Conviction of sin will not occur where the truth is not being preached and taught.

Paul's commitment to preach the Gospel could not be questioned. He worked hard with his hands and suffered reproach for his message. His hope was in God and Christ his Savior. He urged the ministers to continue to preach the truth of the Gospel. Even young preachers were to be an example in their speech, conduct, love, faith, and purity. They were to devote their life to study, urging people to do right, and teaching sound doctrine. He reminded the ministers of the vow they made when they were ordained to be faithful to the Gospel. Paul told them to not neglect the commitment they had made.

They were to practice, cultivate, and meditate on their duties as a minister so their witness would be received well by others. Ministers need to take pride in their teaching and persevere in all things. They are to give of themselves wholly to the ministry so they could save themselves and others.

They are forbidden to rebuke older unbelieving men but must plead with them to accept Christ like they are their father. Ministers are to treat younger men like brothers, older women like mothers, and younger women like sisters. They are to be pure and sinless in dealing with everyone.

Special attention was required for widows who lived alone and had little or no income. It was the church's responsibility to meet the needs of helpless widows. Paul said if a widow had children or grandchildren, it was their obligation to take care of their widowed relative. A true widow who has no support must rely on God to meet her daily needs. When the offspring takes care of their mother or grandmother, the church can then fill the needs of other deserving helpless widows. If a family member fails to meet the needs of a true widow, they have disowned their faith in God through the neglect of their relative who has real needs they cannot meet. Paul said even unbelievers are compassionate and helpful to their relatives.

A widow who lives a life of pleasure and self-gratification is not one the church is obligated to help. She is self-sufficient and can meet her own needs.

If a widow is under sixty years of age or has been married more than once, she is not eligible for help from the church. A younger widow will in many cases remarry so she does not need the support of the church. They may even forsake their faith in Christ to find a new husband. When they withdraw from Christ they may become lazy and be a gossiper and a busybody. Paul's desire was that younger widows remarry, have children, and not give anyone the opportunity to criticize them.

A true widow who needs the church's support is over sixty years of age, has a good reputation through her good deeds, mothered children, shown hospitality, washed the feet of saints, relieved the distressed, and devoted herself to doing good in all ways. These godly widows deserve the church's support. Paul wrote according to the customs and practices in his day when the church met the needs of the destitute.

Elders who perform their duties in the church well by preaching and teaching regularly are doubly worthy of honor and financial support. Paul said the laborer is worthy of his hire.

People are not to listen to a charge against an elder that is brought before a judge, unless there are two or three witnesses. If an elder is found guilty and keeps sinning, they should be punished publicly.

Paul warns against prejudice and partiality. If an elder has fallen away and is being punished, the church is to take their time in reinstating him. Paul said it is acceptable to drink a little wine for the sake of their stomach when they are ill. He is talking about taking a dose *(a little),* not a glass of wine. He said some men's sins will go before them to the judgment seat, but the sins of others will follow the offender to the bar of judgment and be revealed on the Day of Judgment. Our deeds, whether good or bad, cannot remain hidden indefinitely.

Paul's attention now turns to servants and slaves. Servants are to show respect and honor to their earthly masters so the name of God is not disputed or blasphemed. Masters who are believers in Christ are to be respected even more because they are brothers in Christ with their servants.

The minister who does not preach and teach the doctrines of Christ is puffed up with pride, conceit, and ignorance. This results in controversy, disputes, strife, envy, jealousy, quarrels, dissension, abuse, insults, slander, and suspicion. When the truth is taught, we can avoid long-term arguments and friction. Those who do not regard the truth of God can turn their so-called ministry into profit as they encourage people to give to their personal cause and coffers.

Paul reminds us we brought nothing into the world, and we cannot take anything out when we die. We should be content when our basic needs are met. A strong desire for riches has been the downfall of many. The love of money is the root of all evil. A craving for money can lead men astray and cause them to shrink from the faith. The rich have a golden opportunity to be a blessing to those in true need. We are encouraged to flee from personal desires and turn to God. We are to pursue godliness, righteousness, steadfastness, faith, love, and gentleness to find true satisfaction and happiness.

We are to fight the good fight of faith and lay hold of eternal life. Our focus is to be on the heavenly, not the earthly. Paul reminds us of how Christ was sentenced to death by Pilate, but Jesus stood true to God in the face of death. We too are to stand firm to the end of life. Through Christ we are exempt from the second death. He is in a glorified body that shines forth with a radiance that is unapproachable. We give Him honor and praise for His sacrifice on the cross and His glorious resurrection.

Paul issued a warning to the rich to not be proud or arrogant. They must not show contempt to others, or rely on their riches, but on God. Earthly riches are temporal and can diminish greatly or vanish quickly; but the blessings of God are eternal. All good things come from God to His children. The rich are encouraged to share their wealth with those in need. These good deeds create our treasure in heaven that endures forever.

Paul closes his first letter to Timothy by telling him to guard and keep the Gospel message that had been entrusted to him. Timothy was to disregard and turn a deaf ear to worthless babble, godless chatter, and contradictions that are incorrectly called knowledge and spiritual insight. These things lead people away from God and their faith. As he closed his letter, Paul pronounced the blessing of God's grace upon Timothy.

Paul's Second Letter to Timothy

Paul's situation had grown worse. He now sat in prison in Rome with a very uncertain future on earth. We can sense the hopelessness in some of Paul's letter to Timothy. He called Timothy his child and pronounced God's grace, mercy, and peace be upon him. He remembered Timothy night and day in his prayers. Paul wanted to see Timothy very badly as he was very lonely since his friends could no longer visit him in prison.

He recalled Timothy's sincere faith as he trusted completely in God. Timothy's faith was absolute as he trusted in God's power and wisdom. Timothy had been taught the ways of God well by his grandmother Lois and mother Eunice.

He asked Timothy to fan the flames on the gift of God, Jesus Christ. He wanted Timothy to magnify and spread the Gospel to the fullest. God gave Paul and Timothy a spirit of power and love, not a spirit of timidity or cowardice. He knew Timothy had the discipline and self-control needed to go forward with the Gospel. Paul had taught Timothy well. He urged him to not be ashamed to speak up boldly for the Lord or of him as a prisoner. Timothy was to accept suffering for Christ's sake if necessary.

It was Christ who had saved and called Timothy to lead a holy life as he delivered the good news of the Gospel. It was God's grace that enabled him to carry out his ministry. Paul said they did not deserve any merit for their efforts, as their ministry was all about Christ. Jesus came to earth and made death of no effect when He was resurrected. He annulled death and brought life and immortality *(immunity from the second death)* to light through the Gospel.

Paul and Timothy were ordained to preach the message of a risen Savior to as many who would listen. They were like heralds as they delivered the good news to the Gentiles. It was because of Paul's faithfulness to God that he was now in solitary confinement in a Roman prison. Paul made a very strong statement when he said in Second Timothy 1:12: "For the which cause I also suffer these things: nevertheless I am not ashamed: for I know whom I have believed and am persuaded that he is able to keep that which I have committed unto him against that day." Paul had laid it all on the line for Jesus, and he did not regret his commitment. He wasn't ashamed of Christ as he demonstrated so vividly in his preaching. He stood fearless in the face of threats, opposition, and imprisonment.

He told Timothy to hold fast and to follow his example and teaching. His complete faith and love rested in Christ Jesus. Timothy was to guard and keep the Truth that had been entrusted to him through the Holy Spirit. Paul said the Lord had met his needs when certain men deserted him. When his aide Onesimus returned to Rome, he was not ashamed of Paul as he sat chained in prison for Christ's sake. He sought Paul out until he found him so he could meet his physical needs. Paul was very grateful for his friendship and help, and he prayed for the Lord to extend mercy to his friend.

Timothy had tremendous inner strength because his faith was grounded in Christ. He had been instructed in the ministry by Paul, and he was now qualified to teach others about Christian living. He would also train other men as teachers so his work could be extended. Timothy was a very worthy soldier of Christ, but he knew soldiers must bear pain and hardships. A soldier divorces himself from life outside the military as his goal is to please the one who called him into service.

In a competitive game, the winner must compete according to the rules if he is to receive the prize. There are no shortcuts or easy routes as we must stay on the longer and more painful course to compete. Paul told Timothy to seriously consider what he was saying so he would have a full understanding of ministry requirements. He was to preach Jesus as the risen Savior, just like Paul preached. Paul was suffering in chains like a criminal, but he noted the Word of God is not chained or imprisoned.

Paul was ready to persevere with patience and hold on for the sake of God's chosen children. Paul accepted Christ for his salvation, the same as any other person today. Paul said in Second Timothy 2:11, "It is a faithful saying: 'For if we be dead with him, we shall also live with him.'" It takes death to find new life. When we endure to the end we will reign with Him. If we deny and reject Christ, He will also deny and disown us. If we don't believe in Christ, He still remains true and faithful to His Word, for He cannot deny Himself. We are to avoid controversy over words that only weaken and undermine the believer's faith.

Paul said to, "Study to show thyself approved unto God, a workman that needeth not to be ashamed, rightly dividing the word of truth" (2 Timothy 2:15). When we study God's Word, we learn more about Him and His will for our lives. The Holy Spirit can speak to us to lead and guide us based on what we read in the Bible. When we study, we gain confidence and lose any timidity so we are not ashamed of God or His Word. There is no place for empty and vain talk as we are an example of godliness to others.

The teaching of disbelievers will spread like a cancer or gangrene. The false teachers Paul was referring to *(Sadducees)* had strayed from the truth by arguing that our resurrection had already occurred. Christ's resurrection was a fact, but the Sadducees still argued that He did not come forth from death because they did not believe in the resurrection. This weakened the faith of some believers. There is absolutely no value to be gained in a lie.

Paul reminds us that the firm foundation laid by God stands sure and will not be shaken. He said in 2 Timothy 2:19, "The foundation of God standeth sure, having this seal, 'The Lord knoweth them that are his, and, let everyone that nameth the name of Christ depart from iniquity.'" God knows His children by name, just as a shepherd knows each of his sheep. When we accept Christ, we sever ties with Satan and sin. We depart from iniquity to come alongside Christ.

In a large house there are things of value and some that are less valuable, but each item is of value to the homeowner. In God's house, every person is precious in the eyes of Christ regardless of the talents we possess. A person who accepts Christ and separates from the contamination of sin will be set apart and used for good and noble purposes. We will be profitable to Christ, fit and ready to do His work. We are to shun evil and flee while we pursue faith, love, righteousness, peace, and fellowship with other believers. We are to close our minds to trifling things that bring strife and quarrels into the church. We are not to be quarrelsome, but kind and mild-tempered so we can live in peace together.

The teacher must be skilled and able to present his lesson and be willing to suffer if needed. He must face opponents to the truth with courtesy and gentleness, hoping they will repent and come to know the Truth. Opponents may realize where they are wrong and escape from Satan who holds them captive once they see God's truth revealed in us.

Paul said in Second Timothy three that the last days will be filled with stress and peril. People will love themselves and be totally self-centered, lovers of money and greed. Some will be proud and arrogant boasters. They will disobey their parents, be ungrateful and unholy.

Second Timothy 3:3-6 points out the signs of the end time: there will be many without natural human affection, relentless, slanderers, loose morals, haters of good, betrayers, self-conceited, lovers of sensual pleasures rather than lovers of God. They claim religion but deny and reject the power of God. Their conduct tells what kind of person they really are. Paul instructs all believers to avoid these people. They will worm their way into our homes and load us down with their burdens of disbelief. They will try and lead God's children away from Him. Those who are weak spiritually will fall for anything since they are not grounded firmly in the Scriptures. These false teachers are like counterfeit that is of no value.

Timothy had followed Paul's ministry closely. He knew about Paul's commitment to Christ and saw how he was persecuted for his faith. Paul reminded Timothy God allowed the trials to come, but he also provided a way of escape. Paul said all believers can expect persecution. The persecutors will get worse with time, leading as many astray as possible. He admonished Timothy to hold to the things he had learned. Timothy had learned the things of God about salvation as a young boy from his mother and grandmother.

Paul said in 2 Timothy 3:16-17, "All scripture is given by inspiration of God, and is profitable for doctrine, for reproof, for correction, for instruction in righteousness: that the man of God may be perfect, thoroughly furnished unto all good works." We can be thankful for the Word of God that we can study as we strive for perfection. The Word of God is His standard for daily living.

In Second Timothy four, Paul charged Timothy to be a herald and preach the Word. He was to preach with urgency since so many needed to hear his message of salvation in

Christ. He was to preach whether or not the opportunity was favorable or convenient, welcome, or unwelcome. Paul instructed Timothy to call sin by its name and show people the error of their ways. He told Timothy to convince by rebuking, warning, urging, and encouraging them to make a change. Some will not tolerate sound and wholesome instruction. They will want to hear something that is pleasing and does not convict them of sin. They will keep searching for a teacher who will foster their errors and turn aside from the truth. They will wander into myths and fictions, and stray from God's Word. Timothy was to be calm and steady, accept suffering, work as an evangelist, and fulfil the duties of a minister.

Paul knew his days were numbered when he said in 2 Timothy 4:6-8, "For I am now ready to be offered and the time of my departure is at hand. I have fought a good fight, I have finished my course, and I have kept the faith. Henceforth, there is laid up for me a crown of righteousness, which the Lord, the righteous judge, shall give me at that day: and not to me only, but unto all them also that love his appearing." What a strong testimony in the face of death! It should be the goal of every Christian to be able to honestly make a similar statement at the end of life.

Paul wanted Timothy to visit him before he died. He asked Timothy to bring his cloak, books, and parchments when he came. Every person had deserted Paul at his first trial, and no one stood in his defense. The Lord alone stood with Paul and gave him strength as he preached to the Gentiles and endured prison life. Paul was confident the Lord would deliver him from every assault. He would preserve and bring Paul safely to His heavenly kingdom to be with Him in glory forever. Paul prayed again for God's grace to rest upon his good friend Timothy.

Chapter Fourteen

Paul's Letters to Titus and Philemon

Paul wrote a brief letter to Titus and Philemon. Due to their brevity, both letters will be covered in this chapter.

<u>Paul's Letter to Titus</u>

Titus was a young minister that Paul wanted to encourage by writing him. He called Titus a son because of their common faith in the Lord. Paul had left Crete earlier so he could ordain elders in every city where he had preached. Paul also ordained young Titus as a minister earlier.

Paul restates the qualifications of an elder in Titus 1:7-9. These are the same qualifications mentioned in First Timothy three (see chapter thirteen of this book). The office of elder is the high calling of God. It is a call to service to Christ and His church. The elders are to make sure the church thrives under Biblical teaching and maintain order among its members. Paul found it necessary to have elders in each church he planted so he could move on to other areas to establish more churches. Paul was a missionary, not a pastor.

There were many Jewish unbelievers who were false teachers to the new Christians. New converts were called babes in Christ elsewhere. A baby needs the nurture and care of a loving mother, and this is the role the elders in the early Christian churches were to play. They were to confront and expel false teachers from their assemblies so the Word of God would have full effect. These false teachers not only wanted to lead new converts back into Judaism, but they were falsely teaching for profit. The elders were to rebuke the false teachers sharply. They hoped the false teachers might come to Christ when confronted with the truth of God's Word.

The new converts were not to give attention to the Jewish fables and commandments of men that did not align with the truth in the Scriptures. Nothing was pure with the false teachers as their message was based on fables and myths. Their minds and consciences were defiled and polluted by Satan's lies and their own greed. They said they knew God, but their works denied Him. They were detestable, disobedient, disloyal, and rebellious in God's eyes, and in Paul's assessment.

Paul's message was based on the sound and wholesome doctrine that was God-given. Titus was to urge the older men to be serious, sensible, and self-controlled. They should be sound in their faith, in love, and in steadfastness to Christ.

Titus was to ask the older women to be reverent and devout that would bring honor to their service to God, not slanderers or false accusers, and not drink much wine. Paul wanted the women to be sober and be devoted fully to Christ. They were to be good teachers to young women of what is right. They were to teach the young women how to be disciplined and temperate, and how to properly love their husbands and children. The young wives and mothers needed instruction on how to exercise self-control, be good homemakers, and be kindhearted according to the Word of God. The older women were to be living examples for the younger women. They were to let them see truth, good deeds, and pure motives through their actions.

Titus was instructed to be sound, fit, and wholesome so the opponent to the Gospel would be put to shame and could not cast blame on what Titus or Paul said. Titus was to tell servants to honor and respect their masters without talking back. They must not steal but prove their loyalty to their master. They needed to show their master he could rely on them and trust them without any concerns.

Paul addressed God's grace once again. He said God's grace came to deliver people from sin and to bring eternal salvation to all men. His grace trains us to reject and renounce ungodliness, worldly passion, to live discreet lives, and to be spiritually devout.

He then looks forward to the time our Lord will return. He said in Titus 2:13-14, "Looking for that blessed hope, and the glorious appearing of the great God and our Savior Jesus Christ; who gave himself for us, that he might redeem us from all iniquity; and purify unto himself a peculiar people, zealous of good works." Christ has called us out of sin to salvation. We eagerly await His return to rapture His church.

In Titus three, Paul told him to remind people to be submissive to governmental authorities, to be obedient, and do what is right. We are to not speak evil of anyone, avoid conflicts, seek reconciliation, and be courteous to everyone. We are changed when we accept Christ. In our sinful life, we were thoughtless, senseless, obstinate, disobedient, deluded, and misled; but after accepting Christ, we learned of the kindness and the love of God. We are to now pattern our lives after Christ. He saved us, not because of any righteous works we have done, but out of His pity and mercy. He cleansed us with a new birth and gave us the gift of the Holy Spirit through Jesus Christ.

He gave us the Holy Spirit so we can be justified and made right in God's eyes. His undeserved favor made us joint-heirs with Christ to all God's riches in eternity. This fact gives us an undying hope forever. Paul exhorts us to goodness and good works, for this is good and profitable. Titus was to avoid controversy and wrangling about the Law, for these are futile actions that gain nothing.

Paul instructed Titus to expel those in the assembly who cause division. He was to first admonish the wrong-doer twice before dismissing him. If real change didn't occur in the person promoting division, he was to be discharged from the church.

He encouraged Titus to instruct the people in the church to do good works and labor in honorable employment so they could meet their family's needs. There was no room for idleness, laziness, or unfruitful lives.

Paul's Letter to Philemon

Philemon was a man of means from Colosse. Paul had not visited Colosse at the time he wrote to Philemon. The two had probably met earlier in Ephesus or elsewhere and had gotten to know one another. The book of Philemon only has one chapter that mentions Paul, Timothy, Philemon, Apphia, Archippus, and Onesimus.

Timothy was with Paul at one point when he was in prison as they had traveled and preached together. Philemon may have been a financial supporter of Paul's ministry. Apphia was their sister in Christ and Archippus was a fellow Christian.

Onesimus was Philemon's run-away slave who had come to Paul's prison to help meet his needs.

The church most likely had been meeting in Philemon's home. Paul heard of Philemon's love and steadfast faith in Christ. He freely shared his love and faith to the faithful Christians who met in his home. Paul's prayer was that Philemon's faith would produce an appreciation of what we enjoy as beneficiaries of God's grace and love. Paul was encouraged and blessed from Philemon's love for God that cheered the hearts of other Christians. The Christians had been blessed through Philemon's hospitality and generosity.

Paul charged Philemon boldly to keep doing the good work he had been doing. Paul was an old man and a prisoner when he wrote to Philemon.

He appealed to Philemon about Onesimus who was Philemon's runaway slave. Onesimus had been with Paul attending to his needs while Paul was in prison, but now Paul is ready to reluctantly return him to Philemon. Paul also told Philemon he was a prisoner of Jesus Christ.

Paul said if Onesimus owed Philemon anything or had wronged him, to put it on his account and he would pay him. Paul had a lot of confidence in Philemon's commitment to the Lord, and asked Philemon to refresh him in the Lord. Paul looked forward to getting out of prison and going to visit Philemon at his home.

Summary

When we look back on Paul's life, we can only say, "What a man"! He was a persecutor of Christians and had many of them punished severely. As a devout Jew, he thought he was doing the right thing for God and Judaism, but he had a lesson to learn.

His conversion to Christ in Damascus was unusual. Jesus sent Ananias to pray with Saul so his vision could be restored. Christ said Saul would deliver the Gospel message to the Gentiles scattered throughout Asia Minor. Paul started preaching Christ within days after his conversion. He lost no time in going all in for Christ. Many came to know Jesus as their Savior through the preaching of Paul and his ministry partners.

Paul gave the church specific instructions on organization, structure, and discipline. The church is the bride of Christ, so she needs to be protected from false teachers. Paul taught the elders how to maintain order in the church through the discipline of unruly members.

He suffered much for the sake of Christ. Paul never gave in to his many ministry problems but maintained a strong faith until his race was run to completion. He looked forward to going home to be with the Lord.

Paul left us with an awesome hope of our own bodily resurrection and eternity with our Lord. His testimony is still a shining light to every believer today.

About the Author

Don was born at home in Tazewell County, Virginia. His dad was a coal miner and his mother worked hard to raise five children. Our parents had a strong work ethic matched by a tenacious faith in God. Even though resources were limited, our family was rich in love for the Lord and each other.

Don went to business school after graduating from high school. He worked his way through a maze of different jobs from entry level to management. His jobs ranged from administrative positions to vice president of a manufacturer of furniture. Then he went into field sales calling on the military and universities. He was blessed as many doors closed, but just as many better ones were opened by the Lord.

Don has always been blessed to be fully involved in the Lord's work. For many years, he worked in the areas of music, administration, and teaching the Bible. In October 2014, his elders asked him to become the minister of his church and he still holds this position.

His family has gone through several deaths just as others have experienced, but God continues to bless. We have the blessed hope of Jesus' return to earth when families will be re-united and we will forever be with the Lord. We eagerly await His return when all things will be made new.

www.ingramcontent.com/pod-product-compliance
Lightning Source LLC
Chambersburg PA
CBHW062156080426
42734CB00010B/1709